In Praise of

white-washing fences

with

Jim Haynes

A Celebration

In Praise of Joy
white-washing fences
with

Jim Haynes

A Celebration

Edited by Howard Aster

mosaic press

Library and Archives Canada Cataloguing in Publication

In praise of joy : white washing fences with Jim Haynes : a celebration / edited by Howard Aster.

ISBN 0-88962-846-7

1. Haynes, Jim, 1933- --Anecdotes. 2. Publishers and publishing--Anecdotes. 3. College teachers--France--Anecdotes. 4. Authors, English--20th century--Anecdotes. I. Aster, Howard

PN2598.H3915 2005   070.92   C2005-904040-8

Published by Mosaic Press, offices and warehouse at 1252 Speers Road, Units 1 and 2, Oakville, Ontario, L6L 5N9, Canada and Mosaic Press, PMB 145, 4500 Witmer Industrial Estates, Niagara Falls, NY, 14305-1386, U.S.A.

Copyright © 2005, The Authors
Printed and Bound in Canada.
Cover photo by Ewa Rudling
Designed by Josh Goskey
ISBN 0-88962-846-7

Mosaic Press in Canada:
1252 Speers Road, Units 1 & 2,
Oakville, Ontario
L6L 5N9
Phone/Fax: 905-825-2130
info@mosaic-press.com

Mosaic Press in U.S.A.:
4500 Witmer Industrial Estates
PMB 145, Niagara Falls, NY
14305-1386
Phone/Fax: 1-800-387-8992
info@mosaic-press.com

www.mosaic-press.com

Acknowledgements

This book is for all friends wherever they are in the world and especially for a number of friends who are no longer with us:

Catherine Hooper who died in a stupid automobile crash in her early teens,

James Estrada who shared Venezuela and Georgia with me and who was killed in a military jet accident,

"Red" Williams, by an lucky encounter on a bus in Edinburgh, helped to build The Paperback Bookshop,

Sally Belfrage, my hostess in London on many, many occasions, the author of A Room in Moscow and other books and a dear friend,

Monika Vig, editor of Hungarian Orange, killed in an automobile accident one rainy morning in Budapest,

Jonathan Philbin Bowman, journalist extraordinaire, killed falling down stairs in his home in Dublin,

Giles Gordon, Edinburgh man of letters, also killed by falling down stairs in his own home,

Roy Walford, Roderick Macdonald, John Lennon, Lou Casimir, Pearl Padamsee and Ronnie Laing,

Maurice Girodias, one of the most important publishers in the 20th century,

Ted Joans, poet, Shuji Terayama, writer, theatre and film director, Jens Jorgen Thorsen, film-maker, Amram Ducovny, writer, Julian Semyonov, writer, Dahn Ben-Amotz, writer, and Mark Boyle, sculptor,

Henry Miller, Lawrence Durrell, Dorothy Parker, Langston Hughes, Bucky Fuller, Samuel Beckett – all who contributed greatly to my consciousness,

And Tom Mitchell, who, thanks to a chance encounter and then falling in love with Tamara Alferoff, greatly contributed to the creation of the Traverse Theatre in Edinburgh,

And, of course, to my dear mother and father, who made all this possible…

And to Terry Rye, for his technical and editorial contribution for this book, to Josh who worked so hard at Mosaic to make this book come to life, to Susi Wyss, one of the great cooks and great lovers of life, and to Lucy Allwood, for her great sense of humour and positive energy, to Cathy Sroufe Monnet, for staying in my atelier all those years ago and suggesting that she cook for me and my friends, to Antonia Hoogewerf, who is a constant source of joy, to Scott Griffith, for his constant support and editing skills, to John Flattau, for his support and friendship through thick and thin, to Rainer & Sabine Kölmel, who are generous beyond compare, to Michel Puéchavy, for his years of trying to protect me from Emile-the-Rat…

to Karolina Blåberg, John Calder, Stephanie Wolfe Murray, Séamas McSwiney, Martin Lehberger, Sheila Colvin, Odile Hellier, Ernie Eban, Norma Moriceau, Hercules Bellville, Elisabeth & Jaco Groot, Fanny Dubes, Howard Aster, Garry Davis, Joe Francis, Hamida & Colin Gravois, Harry Robinson, E.Y. Meyer, Yohanna Troell, Anne Safford & Michael Hoenig, Elsbieta & Jan Kaczmarek, Yoko Sueoka, Menchu Gutierrez, Jill Adams & Garry Smout, Anthony Pilley, Jaume Subirana, James Emanuel, Meg Bortin, Dan Topolski, Kyle Roderick Goldstone, Barbara Hoff, Ruth Holloway & Martin Burke, Anne & Ricky Demarco, Bojana & Dusan Makavejev, Tim & Dorota Chrisp, Natasha Perova, Tanya & Carsten Hansen, Erich & Brigitte Bernhard, Stash Pruszynski, Jane Alexander, Gosta & Viveka Wallmark, my wonderful son Jesper and all of you who I have encountered and shared tender moments with in this crazy life. Thanks for coming!

Jim,
Paris, 2005

HANDSHAKE EDITIONS

Atelier A2, 83 rue de la Tombe Issoire, 75014, Paris, France, Tel: 01 4327-1767   Fax: 01 4320-4195
e-mail: jim_haynes@wanadoo.fr

A PROGRESS REPORT FOR FRIENDS

Handshake Editions is a small Amsterdam and Paris based kitchen-table literary publishing house. We have been publishing from Atelier A2 since 1980. With extremely small print runs, Handshake sells primarily via mail order to friends concerned with contemporary writing.

We solicit your support. The following is a list of our titles published to date. Many are out of print, but we have an intention to re-publish most of these out-of-print titles.

To simplify our price structure, we will charge $10. for each title, but we will not prevent anyone from ordering copies if this is beyond their means. Nor will we discourage anyone from contributing larger sums. Bookshops may order copies for $6 but payment must accompany the order.

• •

NEW DUCK BUTTER POEMS
by Ted Joans
This collection launched Handshake Editions. When Ted was scheduled to read at UNESCO, I suggested we edit a small collection of his poetry to sell at the reading. We did and he did. And Handshake Editions began! Temporarily out of print.

POEMS OF A WANDERING JEWESS
by Judith Malina
After several editions, Handshake gave the book to Judith Malina to reprint in the USA.

THE PARIS/VENICE POEMS
by Barry Gifford
The Handshake Edition is out of print, but is still available in his **COLLECTED POEMS**, published by Creative Arts Book Company, Berkeley. Barry is the author of a dozen or so books. All highly recommended.

KALI WOMEN AND CABALLEROS
by Elaine J. Cohen
Poetry. A few copies still available.

MERVEILLEUX COUP DE FOUDRE
by Ted Joans & Jayne Cortez
Their poetry in French translation; out of print.

RAGS AND JEWELS
by Sarah Bean
This collection of autobiographical stories has an underground following. It is more or less out of print. (Maybe a dozen copies still available.) A French-language translation has been prepared, but never published. We would like to reprint.

BROKEN UP AND DANCES
by Michael Zwerin
This collection of jazz essays, mainly taken from his *International Herald Tribune* column, was picked up at a Frankfurt Book Fair by Quartet Books in London. Mike transformed the essays into his autobiography, reprinted with a new title, **CLOSE ENOUGH FOR JAZZ**.

WEIRD FUCKS
by Lynne Tillman
Another collection of short stories that is out of print in the Handshake Edition, but they can be found in a new and bigger collection of stories of Lynne's published by Serpent's Tail in London under the title, **ABSENCE MAKES THE HEART**. Good news! Lynne has been nominated for the National Critics Award for her new novel, **NO LEASE ON LIFE** (Harcourt Brace).

Books by Jim Haynes

Traverse Plays
(Penguin Books, London, 1966) Edited by Jim Haynes

Hello, I Love You! Voices from within the Sexual Revolution
(first published in 1974 by yours truly under various imprints)
Jean Lafitte Editions, Almonde Editions, Handshake Editions)
edited by Jeanne Pasle Green and Jim Haynes (translated and
published in French, German and Italian) A semi-pirate edition
published by Times Change Press in California in 1974.

Workers of the World, Unite and Stop Working! A Reply to Marxism
(first published in a bi-lingual English/French edition by Dandelion Editions, Paris, in 1978) Later published in a German-
language edition and a bi-lingual English/Russian edition in
St. Petersburg). A new edition published by Glas, Moscow in
English in 2002.

Everything Is! Soft Manifestos for Our Time
(published by Handshake Editions in Paris in 1980). Later
published in German-language Edition by Volksverlag in 1981.
Translated into French and published in a small edition by
Handshake Editions in 1981. Also Glas Publications in Moscow
brings out a new edition in English in 2002.

More Romance, Less Romanticism
(published in an extremely limited edition by Handshake Editions in Paris in 1982. Currently out of print

C'est Ma Vie, Folks and Thanks for Coming!
A Participatory Autobiography
(published in a 2 volume edition of 25 copies by Handshake
Editions, Paris in 1982) Later published in one volume, and both
cut and extended by Faber & Faber, London in 1984. Faber
(Boston) also published it in the USA. Currently out of print,
but a few copies still available in Paris

Homage to Henry: A collection of essays about Henry Miller edited by Jim Haynes and published by Handshake Editions, Paris in 1980. Re-printed in 1982 and again in 2005

Round the World in 33 Days (published by Glas, Moscow in 2002 In English)

The *People to People* Travel series Co-published by Handshake Editions, Paris in 1991 with Canongate Books, Edinburgh and Zephyr Books, Sommerfield, Massachusetts. Five volumes: Poland; Romania; Czech Republic, Slovakia, Bulgaria & Hungary; The Baltic States of Estonia, Latvia and Lithuania; and finally Russia

Very Rough and Very Self-indulgent Year by Year Chronology (published by Handshake Editions, Paris in 2005)

Co-founder (with Jack Henry Moore, John Hopkins, Barry Miles, Michael Henshaw) of the newspaper, *International Times*, London, 1967 and Member of the Editorial Board of Directors

Co-founder (with William Levy, Heathcote Williams, Germaine Greer, Willem de Ridder, Susan Janssen, Lynne Tillman) of *SUCK* – First European Sexpaper, Amsterdam, 1969

Co-founder (with Jack Henry Moore) and Editor of "*The Casette Gazette – An Audio Magazine*" (Handshake Editions, Paris) First conceived in the 60s; it appears from time to time

In Preparation:

Come Again! Further Adventures of Young Jim Haynes (Volume 2 of the autobiography) from 1984 to present. Handshake Editions

Women's Liberation: A Definition
(Handshake Editions) A one-sentence book with a four sentence footnote by Jim Haynes (to be translated into every major world language to be coordinated with Karolina Blåberg)

Collected Newsletters (Handshake Editions)

Tales of Love, Lust, Adventure and other things: An On-Going Saga (Handshake Editions) Stories from the Sunday night dinners. To be edited by Jim Haynes

Cooking for 100 -- Dinner at Jim's in Paris
(Handshake Editions) Edited by Mary Bartlett, Antonia Hoogewerf and Cathy Monnet (with input from Jim Haynes)

Table of Contents

Preface – Howard Aster

Preface

How to celebrate? How to celebrate one whose endless pre-oc-cupation, or occupation, has been and remains to celebrate?

"Celebrate" – to rejoice… to have a festivity to mark… to observe, such as a birthday… to perform, such as a religious ceremony… to praise publicly…to make publicly known…to proclaim…to extol…

There is value in finding a small way to celebrate Jim. He has done it so long and so often for others and with others.

This volume is but a small token by others to do it for Jim.

Why now? Why this way?

Why not? There comes a time…there comes an im-pulse…there comes an idea…there comes a coming together… and so it happens.

Why a book? A volume because it is both a very public act, accessible to others…and also a very private artifact which one can appreciate and dip into, quietly.

This book is a small gift to Jim, by a small group of friends, colleagues.

There are many, many more friends and colleagues out there and they all are also part of this.

Just a few sketches, chapters, snapshots, anecdotes…but what emerges is a portrait of a man, his times, his efforts, his links and relations. We all have our own portrait of Jim Haynes. But what emerges here is also a Jim Haynes that we all recognize, know and surely, we all love!

For Jim…cheers, l'chaim, bonne santé nasdarovny, salute and for many more!

Howard Aster
Oakville, 2005

The "rhino" with Jim at the entrance to his Paperback Bookshop, Edinburgh, 1961

The Paperback Bookshop – where it all began!

Jim Haynes: The Great Communicator

John Calder

When I first met Jim, in 1959, he was running Edinburgh's Paperback Bookshop, largely specializing, in imported American books, especially 'egghead paperbacks', as they were then called, different from the mass-market imprints of the day in size and price, usually aimed at the expanding university market. They came mainly from university presses, but a few small literary firms as well, such as Grove Press, New Directions and Hill and Wang. I was publishing my own similar series and importing some American ones. I had no difficulty in persuading Jim to open an account and we soon became friends.

On that first occasion, having glimpsed a pretty student walking by, he left me in charge of his shop for twenty minutes while he went out to date her. Soon the shop was notorious, both for its willingness to stock intellectual and often sexually daring titles that the prim Edinburgh book establishment would not touch, and for the friendly and non-commercial atmosphere. Jim handed out free tea and coffee – unheard of in that center of Calvinist scroogeness – talked to everyone whether they were buying or not, and would often lend books that were seldom returned. He had bought the freehold for pennies, had only himself to keep and lived simply. The Paperback, with an old rhinoceros head on its outside, became one of Edinburgh's meeting places for students and lecturers, bankers and accountants who liked books, curious local residents and the lonely, and it was certainly the best pick-up spot in Edinburgh with its permanent party atmosphere which Jim so naturally provided.

When *Lady Chatterley's Lover* was published by Penguin after a notorious show trial, Jim's shop was the natural place to buy it. A lady missionary with a grim face did so, carried it out into the street with fire-tongs and ritually burned it. A passing photographer caught the moment which made the local newspapers.

Then Edinburgh's poets began to hold readings in the shop and this led to Jim agreeing to back *The Howff*, a kind of folk-song night-club, where unfortunately the principal folk-singer ran off with the takings just as it was doing well. This did not deter Jim from persuading Tom Mitchell, an eccentric property dealer who liked to give the impression that he was involved in many secret activities, to let him a derelict old building that had once been a flop-house near the castle on the High Street for a shilling a year. Theatrical friends turned this into the Traverse that half a century later is now one of Edinburgh's civic theatre's, but then with its fifty-five seat auditorium, bar and restaurant, the latter sometimes doubling as an art gallery run by another famous Edinburgh character, Richard Demarco, was soon the center of bohemian Edinburgh.

In 1962 and 1963 I organized two large conferences of writers for the Edinburgh Festival. These were intended to be entertainments to educate the public about the variety and significance of international modern literature, a field in which I specialized as a publisher. Some seventy novelists came to the first and one hundred and thirty to the second. My brief was to make the conferences pay for themselves with box-office money and subsidies, but the logistics of doing this were forbidding. I recruited Jim Haynes mainly to find affordable and comfortable lodgings for these writers, eminent literary figures, many of them elderly who would discuss what they did and why, over a week, in Edinburgh's largest public hall.

Jim found some of the most comfortable homes in the city willing to entertain, and royally, the writers and in some cases their spouses or companions. Class considerations and mutual interests were taken into account: some who might need medical attention were housed with doctors. But Jim also found hosts and hostesses willing to give lavish parties for this number of guests, which inevitably included many of Edinburgh's artists and intellectuals. He also set up a bookshop inside the hall, which at one point was raided by the police as they had been told that there would be a display of 'banned books'. As this turned out to be historical, featuring such books as the *Decameron* of Boccoccio and *Ulysses*, they soon went away. He also found many volunteers to put together a lavish programmed, meet and accompany arriving writers and do the hundreds of the small tasks that would otherwise have needed paid assistants.

Jim Haynes' name is still dropped with baited breath in Edinburgh as the 'founder of the Traverse'. He initially took little part in its activities, but when the inevitable rows and jealousies began he was called in to become chairman and, in practice, its manager. I was also co-opted to find plays to perform and directors to stage them. Soon Jim was getting many suggestions and taking them on impulse more than with caution, sometimes showing an unpopular loyalty to someone whose Jim-derived authority turned the committee against him. The committee itself, mainly professional people who wanted to support the arts and were good at raising money to keep the enterprise going, was in retrospect a good one. They defended the theatre against the constant attacks of the tabloid press against the modern, often daring plays that were performed – not many other British theatres were showing an interest in Beckett, Frisch, Ioneco, Pinter, Brecht at all at that time – and endured Jim's sometimes chaotic management and accounting systems with stoic tolerance. But the days came when the tolerance ran out and Jim resigned rather than compromise.

Attending a conference where Jenny Lee, then Labour's Minister of Culture – in effect the only occupant of that post worthy of the title – gave Jim a lift back to London in the ministerial car, he was able to persuade her to back a London Traverse, at what is now the Jennifer Cochrane Theatre. This made a short splash, being run by two warring directors, each anxious to make his mark through this providential springboard, and by Jim. I was asked to be a fourth member of the consortium, but wisely declined, smelling trouble that soon came. Jim then left and started a series of other enterprises, on IT, a hippy newspaper, called the *International Times* until a law suit made them change it to the initials, The Arts Lab, now legendary but eventually closed for drugs, and UFO, a kind of all-night disco.

All this was very much part of the swinging sixties in which I played little part, being busy with many different activities in publishing and the arts, but Jim was a central figure, disliked by authority and eventually going too far to be protected by Jenny Lee. His problem was his extreme tolerance and many of the people who exploited his reputation and popularity were not in it for liberal sympathies or interest in art forms, but just for personal gain, often without scruple. Jim drifted through this with a flower-power sincerity, often innocent on what was really going on around him.

The time came to move on. Next was Amsterdam, where *Suck* became a publication of all-out sexual frankness with little intellectual content but many orgy photographs, and the Wet Dream Film Festival, which advanced free sexuality even further under the Dutch polity of greater tolerance than could be found elsewhere. Last came Paris where Jim moved in 1969. His usual good luck put opportunities in his way and he was able to get a teaching job with an experimental university, first at Vincennes, then at Saint-Denis, where he stayed, teaching in English, until they retired him. Since then and during all those Paris years he has remained an essential port-of-call for tens of thousands of people from widely-different backgrounds of interest. He is no different from the smiling young American who welcomed me into his bookshop in Edinburgh. Some have helped him through his difficult periods, but many more have taken advantage of him. He is trusted by everyone, but often spreads his own trust unwisely, because Jim refuses all caution and always wants to believe the best about everyone he meets. Many see the world as a wicked place, but never Jim. It is not so much that he is innocent – at his age and with his experiences he could hardly be that – but that he wills himself to be an optimist in the Panglossian sense. He is a good, even in some ways a saintly person who sees the world as he wants to see it and ignores all evidence to the contrary.

I have of course had my differences with Jim. I am fond of good wine and like Nietzche I believe that life without the arts would be a desert. Jim is not so much indifferent to both, but totally without judgement on scales of values where such things are concerned. He likes people and will show some interest in what they like to do and what interests them, but only because he likes the people and wants to like them all. Nobody can ever have a bigger personal address book. And nobody could have a better friend. If the world could be made up entirely of people like Jim Haynes, we could, for the brief span of our lives, know an earthly paradise. Unfortunately he stands alone.

"It is not so much that he is innocent – at his age and with his experiences he could hardly be that – but that he wills himself to be an optimist in the Panglossian sense. He is a good, even in some ways a saintly person who sees the world as he wants to see it and ignores all evidence to the contrary."

John

8

Paperback Bookshop, 1960

D. Bain, John, R. McDonald, J. Quigley, Red Wong and Wayne Threm

LAURELS, CEDARS AND ELMS
To Jim Haynes

Pablo Armando Fernández

Years have elapsed, places and people changed.
Some have already left. Seeds under ground they are,
Ready to sprout again in flowers, fruits and grains.
All seems so far away. And yet, memory doesn't die or rest.
Waken, as a sparrow in flight watches the solid ground,
where its feathers will fall to labor, not to end.
None like that day at Paper Back in Edinburgh
Or was it somewhere else? Were we not branches
Of a blooming, perfumed elm?

Wherever was and when, you seemed to crown
That starry day to light embraced Cultures, thus distant,
close to the promised glow that tie us to dreamed liberty.
I search among the scattered fragments of that day,
Back to the abandoned, muddy site, you found
And with the hearts and minds of fellow students from abroad
that follow your spirit for what might be,
recovered walls to place captured images to stay
as flashes that preserve the struggle against wrongs.

Ten years to fight a tyrant, were shown as visions
that reveal the path to free the human breath from chains.
I have to say that you were in those gone days,
So far away, the elected one to initiate
The long longed embrace to make of us
Laurels, cedars and elms. Allow me words
of care to celebrate friendship and brotherhood.
Since then we have followed your ways nearer
To all your soul fold and grants to be well.

Now I am back to that eternal light that keeps
those gone days alive and there is, Keith
And many others who helped in cleaning that space
To endure passed life. There is Hugh McDiarmid
and we talk about the use of words, so they
would not become as empty creeds, black holes.
You are the star, let us have you as light
That will keep those exposed images
To help us fight for the defense of human life.

Jim in his A2 studio with Jack Henry Moore (the legs in the wall poster belong to Gunnel Bloomberg)

Jim with Anna Luna in Russia, 1985, photo by Roberta
Fineberg

"…we met not so much by chance as by small miracle..that magical 1960 summer in Edinburgh…"

Scott Griffith

Jim and I first met by extraordinary chance. Thinking back to his influence on my own life, I'm tempted – no doubt like scores upon untold scores of others who have known him and are reading this tribute – to say that we met not so much by chance as by small miracle. This is my story, plainly told, of that magical 1960 summer in Edinburgh when I first met Jim.

At the time, having done my military service, I was an undergraduate at Chapel Hill enjoying my first ever visit to Europe, aged all of twenty-three, come innocent from Eisenhower's side of the Atlantic. Part of the travel plan was to be a summer school stint at Edinburgh to gain credits towards my degree back home. We summer students, largely young Americans, were boarded at a university hall of residence.

However, my countrymen, I quickly concluded, were impossibly, unrelievedly bourgeois. For most of that group their greatest intimacy with foreigners was speaking occasionally with the few Continental Europeans on the course. One afternoon, lounging near the main door waiting for tea to be served, our knot of folk was approached by a more casually dressed young man wheeling a bike and offering fliers promoting a new bookshop in town. This was Stás Pruszynski, it later emerged, a Polish decathlon champion who had escaped from behind the Iron Curtain by hiding in the luggage rack of a train.

Stás, I witnessed, was getting nowhere. All the Americans were rudely doing their best to ignore him, as if shunning possible contamination by someone so dressed, speaking heavily accented

English. Clearly, they had better watch out or they would be cheated – rooked, as we said then. Appalled by all this, I made a point of taking one of his leaflets and asking him about it. It emerged that he was helping out his pal Jim, another American, owner of the recently-opened Paperback Bookshop.

Next day after our refectory lunch I found the Paperback – quite near George Square and the Men's Union, on Charles Street, opposite the Charles Tavern. (That entire block, a lively neighborhood fifty years ago, has for years been razed: another arid car park.) Inside there was a low-ceilinged, single room essentially, with bookshelves on every vertical surface and all tight with paperbacks. Casually at the till sat Jim Haynes, the owner, a man destined to become a life-long friend. Meantime, the routine warm welcome and offer of a free cup of coffee would do.

Three or four years my elder, another Southerner, Jim explained that during his own military service he'd been stationed near Edinburgh with the American Air Force and had elected to be discharged in Scotland rather than back home. His present shop, he claimed, was the first of its kind in Britain; it sold nothing but paperbacks. These, often colored orange, were mainly published by Penguin and still a novelty.

That last word, Novelty, could be Jim's middle name. He seemed to sow it, like apple seed, wherever he wandered: a novel idea, a different way of behaving, new friends introduced to each other, a productive, stimulating, fresh take offered on the world and on people. As was soon proved, Jim's brand of novelty became powerfully seductive.

With breath-taking insouciance, in Presbyterian Edinburgh Jim undertook to offer not only cheaper paperback books but a cup of free, instant coffee to customers browsing his shelves. Word spread through the town. Curiosity seekers flocked round. Somehow Jim acquired and each morning hung out by the front door the stuffed head of a rhinoceros. Beneath and around the dark, rather dilapidated head that summer a shifting group coalesced, not all young, not all students, daily appearing there to read, to talk,

14

if there was a guitar sometimes to sing, while sipping Jim's awful instant coffee or bottled beer from the pub across the street sold in what were known as screwtaps.

John the Tinker would squat for hours weaving babies' rattles out of dried reeds with folded beer bottle tops inside to make noise, beside a tall, quiet medical student later to become a distinguished professor of gynecology; Highland Jim who wore nothing but the kilt, would stand across from a guitar-strumming junior-year-abroad American math major later to become a world-famous actress; a gorgeous, Swedish au-pair who did batik work chatted with the California artist she would later marry; a black American student with an Irish name might be arguing with a Scottish art teacher with an Italian name; they came and went, this loose Freemasonry of folk from all over, having in common with each other Jim's influence, the welcome novelty he represented to so many.

First a mere daily visitor, I became, increasingly, an habitué. These were impressive people, far more so than the McCarthy era Americans I was thrown amongst on the summer course. And Jim was not a man who, just because he owned a shop, could be tethered to his till. He would be out meeting people, drumming up business, chasing after girls, planning new projects while trusted regulars took charge of the shop in shifts or hawked leaflets round the town. One bunch recently back from a trip to Moscow claimed that there was now a Paperback Bookshop sticker affixed to the side of Lenin's Tomb.

The group, mostly students with bohemian tastes, and a fair proportion of them Americans, that summer comprised – if I can recall some names – Rod Macdonald, Tam Macphail, Gunnie Moberg, Jane Quigley, Red Williams, Gastrell Riley, Stas Pruszynski, Andrei Malczewski, Ricky and Anne Demarco, Leif Christofferson, Marie Depussé, Emilyann Laurenson, David Baird, David Simson, Mike Maclaughlan, Ben Lassers, Alan Daiches and others, fifteen or twenty interesting young adults who had futures before them which involved more than following the dreary American Dream.

When the summer school ended just before the Festival started in August, the others went home but not I. Put out of the

15

hall of residence, I fell in with some who occupied rooms for free in a university building on Torphichen Place slated for reconstruction. A 1960 squat. It was not comfortable, but comfort was not the point. We were having our minds expanded, sparking off each other, seeing possibilities, being exposed to a way of life beyond that dreamed of back home. The pleasure of such experience is irresistible to some at a certain age, and our Big Daddy was Jim, provider of premises, contacts, novelty and hope.

I discovered French cigarettes, the Festival was kicking off, Rod was writing it up for the print media, Ricky and Tam were exhibiting, Jane was acting in a Tennessee Williams play, there were rehearsals, invitations to private views, stories and music in the back rooms of pubs. Jim planned an exhibition space in the tiny, dank basement of the Paperback, but first it had to be dug out. A handful of us saw to that in shifts, spreading off into the town to scrounge old egg cartons for pasting onto the ceilings as combined deadening and decoration. The first show in the newly dugout 'gallery' was of prints by the French artist Sylvie Connal and ceramics by an American potter whose name I have not been able to unearth, Sheldon somebody-or-other.

Upstairs in the evenings space among the books was cleared for performances of David Hume's *Dialogues Concerning Natural Religion*. Most nights, late, we charged down to the delivery bays at *The Scotsman* newspaper building to catch the reviews of plays/exhibitions/events hot off the press. Harold Hobson, drama critic of *The London Sunday Times*, no less, ignored the official festival plays and devoted most of his review to the Hume *Dialogues* at the Paperback. Word got out that one could buy the notorious *Lady Chatterley's Lover* if one went to The Paperback and asked at the till for *Alice in Wonderland*. The newly published, still-scandalous Penguin edition would be passed over in a plain, brown wrapper; business was brisk.

A brief routine fell into place; bird bath at the squat, to the bookshop for breakfast behind the back curtain where the instant coffee was kept, work in the basement or at the shelves or at the till, companionship outside beneath the rhino head, egg and chips along the road for less than a shilling, invitation to a reading, an opening, a dress rehearsal, a party, an outing, or all those, in the afternoons and evenings, and start over next day. Jim had digs at 1 Doune Terrace and used to speak of his wonder at a capital city's habit of 'rolling up the sidewalks and going to bed after 9.30'; he witnessed it daily on his walk back home to the New Town. Apart from the hotels, there were just two restaurants in Scotland's capital then, *L'Aperitif* on Frederick Street, and the *Café Royal* just off St. Andrew Square.

There were no drugs in evidence. Jim, as he always has, drank very little, didn't smoke, and the rest of us were mainly too poor to do otherwise. We got drunk instead on conversation. We got high on our sense of freedom. It was perhaps this, his mere example, that constitutes Jim's lasting influence on so many. He showed, for example, that it really was possible – why not? – to wear a beard and no tie, daring as it was at the time; possible to decide to go live in another country and then simply to do it; possible to say yes instead of no to life, if that's how one felt.

Festival ended, summer over, new term approaching, yet changes working within one. By the time in 1963 that I came back to Edinburgh to stay – for thirty years in the event – Jim and his new wife, Viveka, had a son, Jesper, and were living in Great King Street. Aspects of the summer of 1960 lived on in the Drama Conference and the Writers Conference, in the starting up of the Traverse Theatre in James' Close off the Lawnmarket, and in Ricky Demarco's exhibitions as well as fringe events during the Festival, but the circumstances had changed, and Jim was already planning great, new things, of which others will write.

Those were the beginnings, as I saw them. We were lucky. I wish that all young people could have the opportunity Jim gave our group to profit from travel, to reassess themselves and the world at the moment when the ripeness is there. Maybe they do. I hope so. In any case, meantime we can remember Jim.

"That last word, Novelty, could be Jim's middle name. He seemed to sow it, like apple seed, wherever he wandered: a novel idea, a different way of behaving, new friends introduced to each other, a productive, stimulating, fresh take offered on the world and on people. As was soon proved, Jim's brand of novelty became powerfully seductive."

"We were lucky. I wish that all young people could have the opportunity Jim gave our group to profit from travel, to reassess themselves and the world at the moment when the ripeness is there. Maybe they do. I hope so."

Scott

MEET THE LEGENDARY JIM HAYNES

BOOKS & BOOKS, Lincoln Road, South Beach
Wednesday 21 September
8:00 PM

In 1961 he started Great Britain's first international paperback bookstore and the TRAVERSE THEATER in Edinburgh. In the mid-sixties he co-founded the ARTS LAB in London and the INTERNATIONAL TIMES. Later came SUCK MAGAZINE out of Amsterdam. He is now teaching SEXUAL POLITICS at the University of Paris and has recently launched a series of travel books that awarded "best new invention in publishing" in England.

Meet the legendary JIM HAYNES. He will talk about his travel books, PEOPLE TO PEOPLE, and lots more.

Jim in his studio in Paris - alone!

A Fortnight In The Life...

"When one's friends hate each other/how can there be peace in the world"
-       Ezra L, Canto 115

William Levy

"Our life has touched on so many points," Jim said, "but I'm a little weak on that time together in London." So when Jim phoned from Paris asking for a contribution to his participatory autobiography I took I.F. Stone's advice – the scoops are in your files. Nothing is easier than predicting the past. Instead of pontificating thusly I decided to look for documents which are genuine relics from the 60s – so you, dear reader, experience it directly. As it is said, we were heroes in those days: we thought we were going to invent a new colour. We did. It was, and is, called psychedelic.

Like everyone else who has been around, I've got a little list. I've also got a trunk in the attic. It's one of those large old-fashioned wooden trunks about three feet high and four feet long with bubbles of metal at the corners. The kind people used for transatlantic boat crossings. In fact, I still have it from when I arrived in Southampton aboard the Queen Mary in 1966. Now it's filled with paper, memos, diaries, notebooks, publications long forgotten. A gold mine for any number of cultural historian and social geographers.

Oh no, I think, do I have to go through all of this?!? But I'm lucky. The archive angel is with me.

Almost immediately I find the membership card – no. 43 – from Jim's Arts Lab. Wow! That's like having been one of the first fifty Illuminati. Skimming further through this paper mess I quickly discover two other items of interest.

The first is Diary notes from September 1967. It was the time when I was editor of *International Times*, and a period when Jim and I began a close cooperation lasting many years. Although Jim is not the only character it does place him in the context of events and people.

So as not to confuse matters, let me say that everyone who knows Jim knows also he does not smoke hash. Indeed, he doesn't smoke tobacco or drink alcohol. At the same time Jim has publically supported the libertarian view – the only thing you really own is your own body; what you do with it is not a proper subject for legislative action.

DIARY

Tuesday, 19 Sept.

Jim and I go out on the town. He says: "You are spending too much time working in the house. Part of being editor is to show yourself around town." We take a taxi to Mayfair, to Huntington Hartford's who is giving a party for Sammy Davis jr. It is obvious the house is seldom used, decorated like an hotel suite. Tonight it's packed. The women are garishly dressed. For the most part they look like merchant's wives, hookers and showgirls. The older men are in three-piece business suits. The younger ones chinless wonders in expensive Granny Takes a Trip gear. Find it difficult to start a conversation with anyone. Plenty of food and drink, however. We wait around for a few hours. Suddenly a wave of excitement flows through the card from the direction of the downstairs entrance. There he is! Sammy Davis. Flanked by Huntington Hartford. Both almost run through the rooms saying: "Hi, there!" and "Good to see you again" and "Yes, we must get together." They press as much flesh as possible then disappear again.

Jim and I leave and take another taxi to Peter Owen's house in Fulham. It's a small publisher's party for one of his authors, the 65 year old Guatamalan novelist Miguel Asturias. Jim tries out his broken Spanish on him. He seems like a nice man. I get into a rather heated discussion with Mario Amayta, an editor of an art magazine.

He has an appointment tomorrow with Jenny Lee, the new Minister of Culture. He is not amused when I ask, what does this have to do with art or culture.

An evening of living Dada.

Thursday, 21 Sept.

Important lunch in an Italian restaurant in Soho with Nigel Samuel, Jim and Tom Driberg (Labour M.P. for Barking). The purpose of the meeting is to ask Driberg to help us find a printer. This crazy law they have in England where the printer can have their machinery seizer if the publisher is prosecuted has made it impossible for us. It's not unlike the licensing law John Milton argued against in his Aeropagetica. We had to walk out of our last London printer when the union refused to typeset an advert for contraceptives.

Driberg tells us he has wasted his life in politics. That there is nothing really do be done in parliament, he stays on merely to be of assistance to people like ourselves. My generalism he says has created "this horrid society".

Jim asks if he will intervene with Woodrow Wyatt on IT's behalf. Wyatt is also a Labour M.P. and the owner of printing companies. Driberg says he will do it.

"I'll phone him right now," he says. A few feet away from where we are sitting there is a wall telephone. He wants to make a point of talking in front of us. While I'm finishing my zabaglione I hear Driberg say: "…also I'm here with a young man whose family you know, but whose name I can't mention on the telephone…" (Meaning Nigel whose father was Nye Bevin's patron and a major contributor to their party in the 50s.) "… and he has agreed to put up a proper bank guarantee to back the payment of print bills."

Over coffee Driberg tells us he will see Wyatt and give us an answer next week. We bring up two other concerns.

One deals with distribution. How W.H. Smith dominates what publications will be available for sale, their insistant refusal to stock IT and others on political grounds even though they sell.

Driberg says that when the Railroad Nationalization Act was introduced into Parliament after the war, he remembers, the Smith family was powerful enough to get a special amendment excepting their newsagents in railroad stations from that Act.

The other main concern is my status as an American and editor of a radical newspaper. The point being that under terms of my visa I cannot enter into employment paid or unpaid. Driberg suggest I keep a false diary which if seized in a police raid might justify my presence on the newspaper as part of a research project, like a businessmen who keeps two sets of books. "You should," he says, "have entries about many different publications so it cannot be said you were engaged with any one."

Oz came out today. Richard Neville phones. We speak about matters of mutual interest: exchange ads; printing; subscriptions. I suggest we organize a National Drop-Out Day. Neither one of us would work. Both of us agree to put notices in our publications. We're quite friendly towards each other, but at the same time each knows the other is holding back information. A tacit agreement to relate as icebergs.

Late in the afternoon I get a phone call insisting I come right away to Joe Boyd's flat on Westbourne Terrace.

"Take a taxi," he says. "I'll pay. You won't be sorry you came."

When I arrive I see Michael Abdul Malik, Jim Haynes, and Caroline Coon. They are all smiling so hard it looks like their faces will break. Each is holding a piece of paper in their hand. I also am given a piece of paper. I smile too. It's a cheque for 500 pounds made out payable to IT. Jim has one for the Arts Lab, Michael for Defence and Caroline for Release. The giver wishes to remain anonymous. The only thing he wants in return, he explains, is an agreement for all of us to meet once a week to discuss issues of interest to the alternative community. We agree. We agree. We agree. We agree.

Tuesday, 26 Sept.

Enormous interest in Aleister Crowley right now. One small mention of him in the last issue of IT acted as a magnet for a bunch of letters. Play a feature. Go to B.M. Reading Room. See the first edition of The Book of Lies. ("Liber 333, the Book of Lies, which is also falsely called Breaks, the wanderings of falsification of the one thought of Frater Perduarbo, which is itself untrue.") Also see his signature where the letter "A" in Aleister is formed as a pictograph for male genitals. Quite by accident, in the coffee lounge downstairs, I see Peter Fryer and Michael Chapman. I think the latter uses the lavatory for his ablutions.

Walk down Museum Street and see Tom Driberg in a bookshop. I stop by to say hello. He tells me he is working there to help out a sick friend. He tells me also Woodrow Wyatt's presses will not print our newspaper. So much for trying to work within the anti-establishment establishment. The bookshop does not carry IT.

Stand evening with Alex Gross and his wife Irene Astrahan. Irene gives me her illustrations for the "Acid Test" center spread.

Wednesday, 27 Sept.

Visit Ed Victor at Cape for Aleister Crowley photos. I can get them pre-publication if I mention their forthcoming book The Confessions of Aleister Crowley edited by John Symonds and Kenneth Grant. Ed seems interested in my doing a book of Ezra Pound's radio speeches. Doesn't know what he's getting himself into.

Walk over to the B.M. Reading Room again. This time to search out sources of an article by John Michell called "Centres and Lines of the Latent Power in Britain." Its either a work of a genius or a madman or both. I went, at least, to see that his sources exist, especially Watkins Early British Tracking and Old Straight Tracks. They do!

Thursday, 28 Sept.

Spend all day inside trying to tie up, mark up, make ready material for IT no.19. And prepare myself for long train ride to printer to Carlisle.

Am I under house arrest?

John Michell phones. He is back in London after rural rides with Sir Mark Palmer and his gypsy band of horse drawn caravans. Also sidetrip to Glastonbury. Wants to come over and tell me about it.

I phone Jim to get the final scheduling for the Arts Lab. He tells me it includes work by the Exploding Galaxy, The People Show, films by Stan Brakage, Storm over Asia by Pudovkin, poetry readings, a special "Black Power Week" programme, Indian music and the European Premiere of Eric Satie's Vexations, a work for piano repeated 840 times by Richard Toop.

"I'll have someone bring it over right away," Jim says. Then he continues: "I had a great day selling IT on the King's Road last Saturday. I met a lot of people and sold a lot of papers."

That's true. Jim must be the world's best street seller.

"Lister," I say. "I have an idea. We can announce it in the issue after this."

"What's that?," Jim asks a little bit suspiciously.

"Let's arrange a non-conference at the Arts Lab. We can call it Ying-Yang Uprising. That's "Ying" not "Yin" after the Coasters record Little Egypt ..."

"Oh you Capricorn Surrealist," Jim replies laughing. "Okay. Let's do it!"

"*So as not to confuse matters, let me say that everyone who knows Jim knows also he does not smoke hash. Indeed, he doesn't smoke tobacco or drink alcohol. At the same time Jim has publically supported the libertarian view - the only thing you really own is your own body; what you do with it is not a proper subject for legislative action.*"

William

2nd INT. PORNO FILM FESTIVAL IN AMSTERDAM THIS OCTOBER

Filmmakers and voyeurs, write S.E.L.F. for details about how to be included in the celebration

6000 YANKEE DOLLARS prize money

« for best films

Sexual Egalitarian & Libertarian Fraternity

Jim Haynes
Atelier A2
83, rue de la Tombe Issoire
75014 Paris France

tel. +331 43 27 17 67   fax +331 43 20 41 95   e-mail jim_haynes@wanadoo.fi

Legendary cultural entrepreneur keeps coming back to Edinburgh for more

By John Morrison

EDINBURGH, Aug 22 (AFP) - One experience of Edinburgh in the festival month of August is enough to last some people a lifetime, but Jim Haynes is clocking up his 48th and shows no sign of flagging.

Haynes, 70, is a genial moustachioed American who first came to Edinburgh with the U.S. Air Force in 1956 and stayed for a decade. A key figure in the underground counterculture of the 1960s, he was friendly with everybody from Mick Jagger to Samuel Beckett.

He opened the city's first paperback bookshop in 1959, founded the legendary Traverse theatre three years later, and helped organise groundbreaking conferences in Edinburgh for writers and dramatists before moving on to London, Amsterdam and Paris, where he now lives.

Haynes can claim to be one of the original pioneers who helped the Edinburgh Festival Fringe expand from humble beginnings to its present size, with some 1700 separate productions jostling for attention over a period of three weeks.

'I think the original spirit is still there,' he told AFP in an interview. Others may look back and claim that things were much better in the olden days when they were running the show, but not Haynes.

He dismisses the annual round of criticism that the Fringe has become too big and too commercial, and that its audiences prefer third-rate standup comedy to highbrow cultural events.

'They have this discussion every year: is the festival too big, are there too many standup comedians, is it out of control, should we have some kind of quality control? It really doesn't matter.' Even bad standup comedy 'adds to the gaiety of the thing,' he believes.

Many of the fringe performances of theatre, dance and other arts may be mediocre and almost all lose money, but he thinks that is secondary to the priceless experience they give to those who take part.

'There is one element that people don't give enough value to, and that is the kids who come here and get experience of doing a production. Even if they get audiences of seven people, I think it is worth it for them. And sometimes by chance they have a hit on their hands.'

This year Haynes has been strolling through the rain between his favourite venues, the Assembly Rooms, the Film House, the Traverse (now a smart professional theatre underneath a modern office block), and the tented city of the Edinburgh Book Fair.

Edinburgh's August arts extravaganza, which now comprises four or five separate festivals, is now so large that there is no single watering hole where everyone meets.

"Memories...Memories...
Unchangeable you!"

Michael Shea

October 1959, and I am a new undergraduate at Edinburgh University. I am in book-buying mode. I am unfamiliar, except for a bookcase full of pre-War and Wartime Penguin orange jackets inherited from my father, with paperback books. Hardbacks were everything. My cousin, Nan Wilson, sends me off to the corner of George Square in Edinburgh, to a new shop, a paperback book shop. "You can't miss it. It has the stuffed head of a rhino outside." I meet an American. He's called Jim Haynes. He had served in the US Army in Scotland in the mid-fifties and he liked the country and the people so much that he had stayed on. He's standing at the door of his shop surrounded by several beautiful girls. He's very like Jim Haynes looks today, forty-six years later: same smile, same moustache (I think) same hairstyle, same charm, same friendliness. Only the plumpness round the middle has been added. Watch it, Jim! Over that first year I go to several play-readings at his shop, drink cups of weak coffee, since I love the atmosphere and the girls. Oh yes, and I buy a few books…

I have a flat above a pub in Rose Street, a narrow lane behind Princes Street in Edinburgh. It used to be a brothel, and it cost me only £800 to buy, complete with its little, barred, speakeasy door inserted in the door. Jim comes around quite often, bringing new friends with him. During one Edinburgh Festival I have to move out: there's a Writers' Conference on at the same time, and, largely due to Jim, Colin MacInnes author of that definitive novel of swinging London, *Absolute Beginners*, and the famous-notorious

29

Norman Mailer become my temporary tenants. I have Norman's book *The Naked and the Dead* dedicated to me, as his "Absentee Landlord". We have a party in the flat one night where I see William Burroughs sniffing white powder up his nose. When I ask about it, I'm told it's a kind of snuff. We were all innocents in those days. I remember a bluff police sergeant arriving at the door late at night and watching curiously as Burroughs sniffed some more powder, then telling us to keep the noise down since we were disturbing the neighbours. There was another incident around that time when John Calder and Sonia Orwell, George's widow, skirmished in a Greek restaurant across the road from my flat, and Jim brought the former over to me to have some blood washed off him. That's how I remember it anyway.

Jim comes past another day. Get your old clothes on, he says. Do you have a big paint brush? We're going to whitewash a large room in a tenement off the High Street. Why? I ask. It's going to be a theatre. A new theatre. An experimental theatre. It's going to be called The Traverse Theatre, since the stage will be in the middle of the room and there are going to be wooden seats tiered to each side. That's how it was. Patrons had to climb over bare wooden boards to get to their places. They put on some pretty good plays. Others have written about all that. I just helped whitewash the filthy walls. In return I have membership card thirty-nine. It should probably be number nine, but they started numbering from thirty to make the numbers look better. And what a huge success the Traverse is today. I went with Jim to other events: for example Marlene Dietrich singing at the Royal Lyceum Theatre (I've just stepped down from being its Chairman) with a noisy man wearing a white suit sitting in front of us, a young man to each side. Yes…Noel Coward.

Jim Haynes has always been the personification of the word catalyst: promoting change without changing himself. And of the word bonding. He bonds people across the world whatever their background. He's always been like that, extending relations across the rusty old Iron Curtain for example, or producing soft core porn magazines to stimulate more than just sexually related feelings. His diaries, shared with so many, bring back memories of so many… places, people, friends, girlfriends. When I left Edinburgh to join the Diplomatic service back in 1963, Jim became my tenant in my ex-brothel flat. We've seen each other pretty regularly ever since, either on his "never-missed-an-Edinburgh-Festival" trips to Scotland, or in Paris for nights on the town or at his Sunday evening parties. They are a bit like the loaves and the fishes story from the gospels. How he feeds everyone when he doesn't even know how many people are coming is beyond my comprehension, yet there's always plenty for everyone. My wife Mona and I have sent more than a few friends to those soirées across the years. When I worked for The Queen at Buckingham Palace, her Principal Private Secretary's daughter was Jim's current girlfriend. I'll leave it to him to tell you stories about the joys of ringing the Palace to talk to her father.

Jim is unchangeable. When he had a small heart attack a couple of years back, he had just arrived in Edinburgh for the Festival, and he went more or less straight into the Western General Hospital. I was one of the first to visit him in his private ward, and there he was, sitting up in bed, flirting with the nurses who were stacked around him in droves. Unchangeable you, Jim…..

"Jim Haynes has always been the personification of the word catalyst: promoting change without changing himself. And of the word bonding. He bonds people across the world whatever their background. He's always been like that, extending relations across the rusty old Iron Curtain for example, or producing soft core porn magazines to stimulate more than just sexually related feelings."

Michael

Jim's son Jesper, his mother Viveka and Jesper's half-sister Lisa, in Stockholm

"Jim simply wanted life to be better and more civilized"

Ricky Demarco

Jim Haynes first entered into my life during the Edinburgh Festival a long time ago when I was walking from an Oxford University Dramatic Society presentation of *Corruption in the House of Justice*. I had seen it with my wife Anne and my sister-in-law Elizabeth. Jim, being one of the few people to own a motor car in Edinburgh at that time, caught up with us as we walked up the Royal Mile. Of course, we had noticed him at the play. He had, even then, that quality called charisma which set him out from the crowd, and his first words were typical. "Can I give you folks a ride anywhere?" Little did I know that it was to be a ride which would completely alter my life. Of course it had to be that he took us to the Laigh Coffee House, and it had to be that we went on with him afterwards to the Central Hall, Tollcross to see another Festival production at midnight entitled *Arlecchino*, performed in Italian.

Jim might have been from another planet as far as Edinburgh was concerned. He was a clean-cut Air Force man from Kirknewton, smelling deliciously of Old Spice. But he certainly was not typical, and it was difficult to believe even then that he was in Edinburgh as part of the American Air Force. He was very much 'at home' in Europe. In fact he had managed to wangle things so that he did not live on the base.

After countless cups of coffee at the Laigh Coffee House there gradually began to develop the idea of the Traverse Theatre and the Paperback Bookshop. Jim's lifestyle demanded that Edinburgh become a better place outside the festival than it had been up to his arrival on the scene. Jim simply wanted life to be better and more civilized, and he knew by instinct that the language of art had to be used.

And so the Traverse was started, not so much as a place for the avant-garde, but as a place for people to meet. Jim has never taken art so seriously that it can become more important than human relations. That was one of the first things I learned from him. Somehow between that first meeting and the opening of The Paperback Bookshop and *the Howff* things very much built up for the Traverse Theatre to become inevitable, and from the moment it opened its doors in 1963 on a cold January evening, the Demarco Gallery was also inevitable.

"Jim's lifestyle demanded that Edinburgh become a better place outside the festival than it had been up to his arrival on the scene. Jim simply wanted life to be better and more civilized, and he knew by instinct that the language of art had to be used."

Ricky

Paula Klein, Jim, Asa Tolgraven in Edinburgh, August 1983, photo by Jesper Haynes

Catherine Monnet with her mother, Marguerite Sroufe and Jim.

"He was utterly unlike anyone else: laid back, sardonic, with the quality he's retained throughout his life"

John Lloyd

I knew Jim as the owner of the Paperback Bookshop in Edinburgh, when I went there to University in 1964. He gave a talk at Freshers' Week - the day organised for first year students, designed to give the new boys and girls some sense of the university and its society. He was utterly unlike anyone else: laid back, sardonic, with the quality he's retained throughout his life - of a kind of innocent amazement that anyone would wish anything other than freedom to do as s/he wished.

This was utterly beguiling to some of us - though it has to be said it was a minority. Edinburgh was a relatively conservative university then, and later: those students who were radical in their opinions and lifestylke were a minority, even within the arts and social sciences. It was a university strong, above all, in medicine: it was one of the premier medical schools in Europe. And it was strong too, in physics, chemistry, engineering and computer science - the last of these just beginning. The students in these faculties worked long hours, and had little time for radicalism. Further, radicalism then often meant Marxism or - a little later - Scots nationalism: Jim was benign to both of these delusions, but never part of either's gangs.

He was in the tradition, then young, of American beat-cum-hippiedom - without fully being part of either. He had and retained as his prime mover an interest in literary and dramatic entrepreneurship: and his achievements - through the *Paperback*, the *Traverse Theatre*, the *Arts Lab*, *International Times*, *Suck* and his voluminous self-revelatory writings, as well as his sponsorship of countless artists and his provision of spaces within which art and drama could find its own level – were very large.

The list of his creations – incomplete – reveals a paradox which those of us who are glad to have known him over the years find ever puzzling, and constantly admirable. He created much, but didn't claim anything. He built, then moved on. If it weren't slightly absurd to use the word of a man so delighting in the joys of the flesh, he had a priestly quality – the best of priestly qualities, an ability to renounce what he had made. Not just an ability, but, it seemed, a compulsion.

Jim is a man of value because he seemed to know his own mind,and thus be able to make his own way, from an early age. he seemed to have worked out what his life would consist of – and then take care to make it so. I say 'take care' – it was never obvious. To those who knew and admired him, but were never close to him – like me, and I guess many thousands of others – he preserved the air of causal ease, open to all suggestions, free from all entanglements except those which would give most stimulation.

He came to Moscow several times, when I was there. I introduced him to a friend of mine who taught English to students at Moscow State University – a lady then in her seventies. She was charmed by him, and asks after him still: her students were even more so. Part of it was his frank interest in women: part of it was his frankness, and his interest. May he live long: he's a kind of example, and such men, though they can be dangerous, are also valuable.

"The list of his creations - incomplete - reveals a paradox which those of us who are glad to have known him over the years find ever puzzling, and constantly admirable. He created much, but didn't claim anything. He built, then moved on. If it weren't slightly absurd to use the word of a man so delighting in the joys of the flesh, he had a priestly quality - the best of priestly qualities, an ability to renounce what he had made. Not just an ability, but, it seemed, a compulsion."

John

Jim with Carol Stewart at the Frankfurt Book Fair

A quiet moment with Paula Klein at A2

"...still putting their trust in the human race..."

Irving Wardle

It made all the difference that it happened in Edinburgh. I started going up there in 1963 as a theatre reviewer for the *Times*. My predecessor on the paper had a strong, if unoriginal, opinion about the place – "I've been going to Edinburgh for twenty years, and I've always hated it", he told me; "the buildings frown at you." The first time I elbowed my way through the Princes Street throng to the wail of the Waverley Station piper, I saw what he meant. All efforts to create a festive atmosphere had failed to dispel the spirit of John Knox and Highland knitwear. And how could you have a great city without a river?

By this time, Jim Haynes had already launched his Paperback Bookshop in Charles Street. Books were off my beat; but, after one frozen look at the official festival programme, I made off to his recently opened Traverse Theatre, then situated in a tumbledown ex-dosshouse in the Lawnmarket in the old town. It too was crowded. But I can think of no greater contrast than between the tourist hordes oozing through the intestine of the Royal Mile and the sharp-eyed kids who peopled Jim's establishment For one thing, they didn't seem like a crowd; they were so much at home there that no matter what the numbers there always seemed to be plenty of space. They came in at street level and took the spiral stone stairs the theatre (70 seats) where they might find a rarity from the nineteenth century German repertory or a brand new multi-author piece about motorway sex. The next flight led up to Ricky Demarco's gallery (another wild flower growing out of the Edinburgh rock-face); upwards again to a bar, lounge and restaurant, all open day and night like the theatre; and thence to a Stevensonian labyrinth including overnight pads for friends and performers, like the Spartan cell I once crammed into with the bulky Declan Mulholland for a point-blank recital of blood-curdling IRA ballads.

Such was Jim's domain before anyone had started applying the word "alternative" to what was going on in our cities. It was most visible of all in Edinburgh because – apart from Henderson's wonderful salad bar - there was nowhere else to go after dark. Outside the Lawnmarket lay a desert of Presbyterian granite, as unwelcoming as a bank vault. Inside, there was friendliness, art, every chance of a pickup, and a cuisine purged of Hiberian carbohydrate. I don't remember anybody dancing, there wasn't room for it. But anything else you might want from human society was there.

In the only conversation I remember with Jim from this time, he told me that his operation had nothing to do with the Edinburgh International Festival. Rather it was built on Edinburgh's status as a folk-song capital, and it was the folk audience he wanted to attract rather than people who'd missed the boat for the King's Theatre or the Lyceum. In his book *Thanks for Coming!* he records the tensions and daily tasks of running the Traverse. All that was invisible to his public. What we saw was a relaxed figure moving through the party as though he had all the time in the world and could imagine no greater pleasure than being there: as you might imagine the Pied Piper once he had spirited the children of Hamlin into the mountain.

Around this time Joan Littlewood, then laying plans for her Fun Palace, saw Jim as a kindred soul and sought him out as a potential ally. The Fun Palace famously never happened; but if it had come true, I cannot imagine Jim having much to do with it – because the nature of Littlewood's genius lay in judgment and control. As she saw things, if people were in a fun palace they should be having fun: that was what is was for. Whereas Jim's position – and offhand I can think of no other public figure who has fully shared it – was to relinquish judgment and control, unless his own colleagues started turning into control freaks. Where others would look at a situation and see a thousand problems, Jim had the faculty of cutting straight to a simple solution. And by some prelapsarian fluke, he was born with a trust in the human race as a positive force that needs no authoritarian restraint. His entire creed is in the statement: "I think that people should be brought together and that we have to create environments and situations to bring people together." After that they can be left to make something good out of it. His unique achievement over the past 45 years has been to create a series of spaces where this has happened.

Sometimes it has led to unlikely friendships. As with the veteran Romanian director Radu Penciulescu who was rehearsing Brecht's ruthless *Lehrstuck , The Measures Taken*, for the Traverse where he met an English Army Major with whom he got on like a house on fire, partly thanks to their shared passion for pipe-smoking. The Brecht, when it opened, was unsurprisingly greeted with loathing by the reviewers who saw it as a cruel example of boy-scout Marxism. But on his way to the Lawnmarket next day, Radu encounted the Major who sprang to the show's defence. He absolutely loved it, he said, enjoyed every minute; these reviewers are idiots, they've no sense of humour, they take everything so seriously. But you and me, we know it has nothing to do with life, it's just entertainment!

That little story reflects a long-standing argument over Haynes enterprises. On one hand - if bringing people together is the main thing, that means criticism is switched off so what's to stop bad art from taking over? Everyone is beautiful and all shall have prizes. On the other hand, what does the quality of a work matter so long as it expands the boundaries of friendship? On grounds of scarcity value alone, I side unhesitatingly with the second argument. There are always hordes of bitingly intelligent players squabbling over the traditional territory; but precious few who know how to switch the critical faculty off and enlarge the territory. Another great liberator, Schiller, famously described the experience of having a censor watching at the gate of the mind, who has to be put to sleep if the imagination is to smuggle out anything of value. That image could have been coined for the Travese Theatre, which combined prodigious productivity (some 17 in-house productions a year, not counting performances by visiting companies) with work of immediate and lasting value, much of it by untried young artists who needed no managerial supervision.

When Jim transferred his operation to London in the late sixties, everything that was true of the Traverse was equally true of the Drury Lane Arts Lab – except that, merged into the now booming alternative and fringe theatre scene, it did not stand out in such bold relief as in Edinburgh. Before the Arts Lab came the transfer of the Traverse company to the Jeannetta Cochrane Theatre in Holborn, a move smiled upon by the Arts Council but much disliked by Jim who found himself for the first time saddled with fixed routines and commercial budgeting, all for a cold unconvivial venue where the only thing for an audience to do after the show was to go home. It has to be said, though, that his collaboration with Charles Marowitz at this unloved address yielded some of the best remembered work in the company's history, including the production of Orton's *Loot* which conclusively put that masterpiece on the map after its failed regional tour. As a reviewer, I was programmed to be more aware of the Cochrane, where shows were announced and ticketed in advance, than the Arts Lab, where the night's offerings were written up on a blackboard at the last minute like menu specialities. But it certainly pulled people together. I recall two evenings in Drury Lane; one at a flat further up the lane where audiences of around 10 were invited to tea with Miss Gentry, a hat designer who lived there and was happy to hand the scones round and tell these parties of strangers about her life. "We're on an actuality kick at the moment", was Jim's take on this event. Another night I went along to the Arts Lab itself in company with the insatiable avantgardist Margaret Croyden. The place was packed. We sampled some New Age food, inspected the cinema (no seats for the audience, just a wall-to-wall foam rubber mattress), and finally attended one of the absurdist pieces of John Grillo of which all I remember is the sight of Grillo playing a ragged old man in a very hot room. Then we went out into the street. "Well," Margaret said, "You wouldn't find Walter Kerr going to a place like that." It was a typically unanswerable remark. On another occasion I met her climbing the desert slopes of Persepolis, Iran, to see Peter Brook's *Orghast*. She was wearing a cocktail dress. "You filing tonight?" she asked. Margaret was the polar opposite of Jim. She carried Manhattan with her wherever she went: he could have made the Garden of Eden blossom in Times Square.

I lost contact with Jim when he left England after his two years at the Arts Lab. Rumours drifted back of his underground Press exploits in Amsterdam and his philosophy classes at Vincennes, but it was only from the late eighties that I caught up with him again, first on his annual returns to Edinburgh and then at his Paris house. Now, instead of being the centre of a crowd, the heat was off, and when we met it was to wander the streets which were full of memories for Jim; or sit in his living room in the rue de la Tombe Issoire where he would talk about his *People to People* travel guides, his plans for a Paris Arts Club, the discovery under his floorboards of a secret cellar dug out during the Occupation to shelter fugitives from the Germans, the craziness of his publisher friend John Calder who was still humping suitcases of books around to clients in his seventies; and, of course, about his Sunday night open dinners where all the world can come to Jim's house. Later again, my daughter went to live in Paris where Jim looked after her until she got herself launched. The most useful thing he gave her, she told me, wasn't the hospitality but the motto: "happiness is an intellectual decision."

By this time Jim had suffered some painful setbacks in his life, none of which dented that resolution. The first half of his life is spectacular. The second half is heroic. You can't count the number of counter-cultural flag-wavers who were around in the sixties, most of whom turned into suburban office-workers once they found they were living in a condemned playground. The test that Jim and a few others (like Calder) passed, was to ignore the passing of the sixties and live on with the same generosity and hopeful energy, still putting their trust in the human race so that when you find yourself in their company you feel quite pleased to belong to it yourself.

"Jim had suffered some painful setbacks in his life, none of which dented that resolution. The first half of his life is spectacular. The second half is heroic."

"The test that Jim and a few others (like Calder) passed, was to ignore the passing of the sixties and live on with the same generosity and hopeful energy, still putting their trust in the human race so that when you find yourself in their company you feel quite pleased to belong to it yourself."

Irving

Dusan Makavejev and Jim in Edinburgh

Jim HAYNES
ATELIER A2
83 rue de la Tombe Issoire
75014 Paris, FRANCE

Poznan, Sept 24 1987

Dear Jim Haynes,

On behalf of Teatr POLSKI w Poznaniu, we are
inviting you to realize a videoprojection of the "Orchestra
of the Eighth Day's" new performance called "One Man Symphony".
The performance will take place between November 20 and December 20.
You will be provided hotel accommodation and daily allowances,
and we will cover your travel expenses.

We are looking forward to seeing you in Poznan,

Kindest regards,

Jan A.P. KACZMAREK
Orchestra of the Eighth Day.

Z-CA DYREKTORA
Jan Harajda

48

"...bringing people together, building bridges between East and West. And it worked!"

Stephanie Wolfe Murray

Jim's reputation was what I first heard about, not the man himself. It was the early 70s and I lived near Edinburgh in a small, dilapidated 19th century Scottish castle. Largely because of my sudden and intense involvement with Canongate Publishing, my own family life was falling apart too.

It was still the hippy era although I had given up wandering about in bare feet and it was around this time that I heard about Jim. He had a formidable reputation – founder of Britain's first paperback bookshop, and founder of the Traverse Theatre, both in Edinburgh. He also began *Suck* magazine in London, and God knows what else, although I shouldn't bring Him into a piece about Jim. His reputation had an aura of sexual freedom about it. Forbidden fruit.

When I finally did meet Jim in 1975 it was through John Calder (of course) at the Frankfurt Book Fair. We got on famously from the start but I avoided him too as I couldn't stand the thought of some orgy in an underground cavern. My life had enough complications of its own. How silly I was! After all these years, there is no one I trust more.

So skip at least ten or fifteen years, years in which I saw Jim at Frankfurt, and in Edinburgh at the Festival. We kept in touch and our friendship grew. We started a habit of giving joint Festival parties; I was there for his first Frankfurt Kunstlerkeller annual get-togethers. What a brilliant host he was, bringing people together from all over the world. He listened and he helped and most importantly, he introduced. I knew what he did for people in the old Soviet Union and other Eastern European countries, and I know how many of them are now established in the West, in many cases living out their dreams.

One hot summer's day in the late eighties I was cruising down Lothian Road, past the main Edinburgh Film Festival venue. There was Jim on the pavement so I stopped the car and told him to get in. "Why don't we do a book project together?" I asked. "Sure darlin', why not?" And so the *People to People* series was conceived.

During its gestation I often wondered and worried about what could happen to hapless travellers who might choose to visit dubious people listed in the books. How could we monitor? How could we check up that all the contributors were genuine, or normal and reliable? Would we be sued if someone was raped or had all their possessions stolen? Jim was sanguine about it all. He has this trust in human nature which, as it turned out, was not misplaced. Perhaps I should explain more to any unfortunate person who does not know about this series. The sub-title of each book gives a quick but succinct summary: GUIDES FOR THE REAL TRAVELLER. They most certainly were not Travel Guides. They were guides to people. I remember him saying to me that it seemed strange to him that anyone should want to go to a country and never meet a local other than the waiters in the hotel. You eat there, swim there, sleep there, trudge dutifully around some galleries or museums and then you go home having met no one who means anything to you. No lasting friendships. To quote from the Introduction of his first book: 'This series of travel guides will contain none of the usual tourist information. . . no museums or galleries, no lists of hotels or restaurants, no suggestions on what to see or to do, and no potted histories.'

OK. So what are they? 'Instead we introduce you to over 1000 individuals who live, work, and play in the villages, towns and cities of the country. . . they want to meet you and to show you how they live, introduce you to their favourite restaurants, share their friends and their interests with you.'

We started the series with two books in the same year, 1991: first Poland and then Romania. We found a small publisher in the States, Zephyr Press, to join us and both editions were printed in Poland. To us they were precious little books, printed on horrible paper, very amateur looking, hundreds of lives crammed into the pages giving the contributors hope of some contact with the outside world. But somehow they suited their genre. I hasten to add that the next batch in the series was smartened up and had a more sophisticated typographical design, thanks in large part to Ed Hogan, the American publisher. He had the guts and, dare I say it, the vision, to join us in the series. I mean what sane publisher would want to publish a list of people? They have now become rare books and are selling for up to £50, if you can find them at all. Soon after the series was completed, Ed died with his wife and step-daughter in a canoeing accident. What a loss. He published *The Complete Works of Anna Akhmatova*, with Canongate as his UK co-publisher. It was a peerless work. Jim and I often talk about Ed and bemoan his loss.

Two books containing three countries in each came next: first Czech-Slovakia, Hungary, Bulgaria, followed by the Baltic Republics: Estonia, Latvia, Lithuania. Finally, in 1996 we published Russia. What a task it must have been for Jim, but as ever he made it look like a stroll in the park.

Why Eastern Europe? As most readers will know, Jim was deeply involved with many people in these countries. He never went there with his hands empty and never lost touch with them. They needed help and moreover, from a practical point of view, they didn't move house too often, if ever, so we knew the books would be useful for a long time. They are still in use and Jim continues to receive mail from users all over the world It really is extraordinary..

He had planned to do France next, possibly Yugoslavia, but it was never to be. For me, I am happy that the series had this Eastern European identity. It was the wackiest project I'd ever been involved with and I too had contacts and subsequently family in that part of the world. Jim and I had many concerns in common. In 1992, halfway through the series, he received an award from the Institute of Social Inventions. Encouragement indeed for someone who had always operated outside the conventional rules of engagement.

You may well ask how Jim found one thousand names throughout these countries. Well, he has a very big address book, so this was a start. He was known there as a philanthropist (and lover of beautiful, talented people) and his name would be passed from one person to another as someone who might help and this he so often did, in a quite bizarre variety of ways. His Paris atelier was open to everyone and anyone. So he already had a foot in the door of Eastern Europe, a vast swathe of mysterious countries whose curtain was being slowly lifted.

He would be given a large space in one of the countries' main newspapers, sometimes as much as half a page, in which to advertise. Readers who wanted to meet foreigners, and maybe make a bit of money by renting out a room, would be invited to send their details to him. They would be asked for their age, address, telephone number, profession, languages spoken, type of housing and brief description of their area in the city or countryside; their 'collectables' (stamps, coins, LPs, CDs, that sort of thing), what languages they spoke (a minimum of two was required and almost all spoke English), perhaps a couple of sentences about themselves, and most importantly, their passions (literature, theatre, cinema, fishing, music, camping, whatever).

I cannot think of a single thing that sums Jim up more than this series although I guess his Sunday night dinners operate on similar lines. But *People to People* reached so many individuals, not just in the capital cities in nine isolated countries, but from towns and villages too. Implicit in the idea behind the books was that the visitor would also be willing to reciprocate should they wish to visit the West. It was about bringing people together, building bridges between East and West. And it worked. It was practical and positive. Things happened to people as a result of using these little books, whether as a contributor or a traveller. He received a letter from a man in California who was planning a project in Romania. The guy had contacted all the official sources to facilitate this – without success. It was only when he was offered a choice of 25 engineers in Romania, one of the books in the series, that he received the information he needed and was able to start work there. Similarly there was an architect needing to do a project in Poland. He contacted Jim who was in the process of preparing the book for publication. Jim looked up 'architects', sent details to the guy and his project was on the way.

A woman in Estonia wrote Jim a beautiful letter telling him about her new friends in London and Chicago who she now corresponds with and of the wonderful summer she spent in the north of England – all as a result of the series. Another man wanted to invest in Eastern Europe and was given useless information from the most obvious sources. Then he saw the *People to People* series in LA and found all the information he needed.

I will give you a taste of some of the enticing entries from these little books. "I am an Associate Professor at the Department of Social Psychology, Sofia University. I love visiting icon exhibitions and watching Nestinars' dancing (girls dancing on live coal)." And from Georgi Chorev: "I love singing folksongs. I am afraid of solitude. I want always to be with friends. I often ponder what love really means". "Let's dance!" wrote Eric Leftimov. Wesselina Geneva tells her readers: "We have a little summer house in a beautiful gorge and we spend all our holidays there". A doctor of medicine writes, "In my free time I write short stories. . . I am attracted by everything beautiful and not least of all by beautiful girls (although I am married)".

An entry that intrigued me was from a composer, Zhivka Klinkova, born in 1924: "I have written 11 ballets, 4 operas and a musical. I have my own ensemble now called 'Bulgarian Baroque' consisting of 6 singers and an orchestra." I had always wanted to go and meet this woman but never did. I wonder if she is still alive. Pavlin Bankov was "born when the second moon of Jupiter was setting. I am trying to preserve the child inside me but that's difficult. My dream is to see the dark side of the moon".

The series received rave reviews. One of the early ones was a four page article by Nicholas Lezard in the *Sunday Independent Magazine* from 22 March, 1992. He had contacted some of the entries in Poland in order to go there to write his review: "The only miserable thing that happened to me in Poland was my departure. I wondered if there was some way of swapping the Polish and British population. Imagine if Britain was full of people who would a walk a mile in tight shoes to do you a favour. It's not simply economics. Several times I had to argue tiresomely with them just to buy them a drink."

In these books Jim shared his gift for friendship far beyond his already wide circle. The contributors to the *People to People* series grabbed the chance to do the same. Jim always disliked having a nationality saying he was an Earthling (he's a great inventor of words). Well, I want to be an Earthling too.

"What a brilliant host he was, bringing people together from all over the world. He listened and he helped and most importantly, he introduced. I knew what he did for people in the old Soviet Union and other Eastern European countries, and I know how many of them are now established in the West, in many cases living out their dreams."

"Jim always disliked having a nationality saying he was an Earthling (he's a great inventor of words). Well, I want to be an Earthling too."

Sephanie

Jim Haynes
Atelier A-2 - 83 rue de la Tombe Issoire
Paris 75014 France
Tel 01 4327 1767   Fax 4320 4195
e-mail: jim_haynes@wanadoo.fr

Letters to the Editor,
The Scotsman,
20 North Bridge,
Edinburgh EH1 1YT   7 September 1999

      After spending three delightful weeks in Edinburgh where I recently attended my
43rd International Festival, I wish to express my appreciation to everyone in Edinburgh
for all the joy this festival produces for me. I think I can speak as well for the thousands
of visitors to your city.

      I hope I am not out of place when I also express my alarm to the City Fathers over
the callous treatment of William Burdett-Coutts and the future of the Assembly Rooms
under his stewardship. Mr. Burdett Coutts has never failed for nineteen years to create a
valuable and exciting theatrical space in the Assembly Rooms. Instead of threatening
him with eviction, he should be supported and encouraged to make the Assembly Rooms
the special place that it has always been under his direction.

      I might add that Edinburgh would be richer if a permanent home could be
arranged for Richard Demarco and his creative surprises.

      I intend to travel to Edinburgh every August from wherever I am on this planet
and I fully expect to attend a festival that has William Burdett-Coutts creating something
in the Assembly Rooms and a corner for Richard Demarco.

Yours sincerely,

Jim Haynes,
Founder,
Traverse Theatre

by Susi Wyss

"Too much and too little, too good and too bad."

Lynne Tillman

Jim is an optimist, he's eternally sure that good will come one day and waits for it. When bad arrives instead, he's sad. His sadness is something like that of an innocent.

Here's a story: When I arrived in London in 1969, I went to the Arts Lab, and, as an eager, English Lit major, and hopeful writer, I asked Jim Haynes if I could set up a lecture and poetry series. Jim said, Yes. Jim would say Yes to almost everything, because he feared conflict, I'd realize later, so Yes, he said Yes to me. He was very shaggy. Actually he didn't say Yes exactly, but nodded solemnly and closed his eyes. I had the feeling he didn't want to know too much about it, in case it would be a disaster.

New to London, I didn't know anyone, so I asked Jim for a list of fascinating thinkers and writers to contact. One of the names he wrote was "Alex Trocchi." A novelist, he told me. I'd never heard of *Cain's Book* or Trocchi, had no idea he was considered by many in the UK one of the worst characters ever, evil, actually, and that he, more than Burroughs, was believed to have single-handedly made heroin cool in London, turning on the young, getting them strung out, and also that, because of this, he was almost never seen in public.

Soon I telephoned Trocchi's number, and Trocchi was friendly, but he paused after I asked if he'd do a lecture or reading at the Lab, and then he said Yes. But everyone must be there, he said. It was a command. He asked me to come to his house and discuss it. His wife Lynn met me at the door, and we went through his address book; she told me the names and numbers they wanted there: Burroughs, Kingsley Amis, Anthony Burgess, and more. Lynn repeated, Everyone must be there. We settled on a date, and she gave me his little black book.

I began calling the names in Trocchi's battered address book, many people were dead, Burgess had moved to Malta three years before, his housekeeper said. Kingsley Amis...I forget where Kingsley Amis was. Burroughs said, in that laconic voice, Yes, and R.D. Laing, too, though I don't remember speaking to him, maybe to his assistant, or maybe I never did. But he was there.

I phoned Kingsley Hall. A man answered, and we spoke for a while; I told him what I was doing, who else was being asked, that I was creating a series at the Lab, and he too was friendly. Then I said, warmly, or American-like, "I hope you'll be able to attend, Kingsley." Instead of saying Yes, he asked me where I was living, and if I needed a place. I said No, that I had a place, that my boyfriend and I had a room in Balham. Then he invited me to a party, I said I'd be there. (I did go, and that's another story.) It was then that I discovered from Jim, this man was named Jim too, that Kingsley Hall was an institution, not a man like Kingsley Amis.

I reported the conversation to Jim, who laughed for a long time, because it was R.D. Laing's and David Cooper's sanctuary for schizophrenics. Now he realized that I was actually going ahead with my plan. So, not long after, he informed me he would be out of town for Trocchi's event. Later, I realized, he was leaving town or going into hiding because of it. Jack Moore, the Lab's other director, also refused to be involved, but he was around that night. Every junkie in London, too. And yes, Burroughs, Trocchi, and Laing were all onstage in Theater One. It was an astonishing sight.

When our two hours had elapsed and I had to clear Theater One for the next event, a play at 11 pm, I ran to Jack Moore for help. Jack told me he wanted none of it, I was on my own, so fearfully I walked up to the stage and told Burroughs and Trocchi that I was sorry, but I had to ask them to move to the cinema. With no resistance, they did -- Laing, Burroughs, and Trocchi, the audience, everyone followed me to the basement, to the foam–rubber floor cinema, the soft cinema.

Jim returned from Sweden -- by then I figured Sweden was North London or Knightsbridge where he was in hiding -- and laughed a lot when I told him I was also followed around all weekend by a junkie named Phil who wanted to move in with me. I explained to him it was impossible, I had a horror of needles, I would faint when he shot up. Perfect, Phil said, it'll make me quit. Jim laughed even harder, and then he made his classic gesture or response: Jim smiled wanly, shut his eyes, and shook his head from side to side, as if the world and everything in it was both too much and too little, too good and too bad.

"Jim is an optimist, he's eternally sure that good will come one day and waits for it. When bad arrives instead, he's sad. His sadness is something like that of an innocent."

"Jim laughed even harder, and then he made his classic gesture or response: Jim smiled wanly, shut his eyes, and shook his head from side to side, as if the world and everything in it was both too much and too little, too good and too bad."

Lynne

Jim at the entrance to his Paris studio A2. Photo by Karolina Blåberg, March 2005

"...someone as unique, eccentric and generous as Jim"

John Flattau

It is difficult to write briefly about someone as unique, eccentric and generous as Jim. Perhaps a way to understand him is to visit him at his Atelier, struggle up to his bedroom/office on the first floor, and ask to see his address books. Which ones he might ask, as he opens his desk drawer to display thirty or forty address books, each two to three inches thick, all filled with names, addresses, phone numbers, and in some cases small notations. They are arranged by country and each book is arranged alphabetically. He actually knows all these people. Another way would be to sit down, take a great deal of time, and read through his newsletters. They are an autobiography in astonishing detail, his newsletters. There won't be a trip you won't believe you were not on, a dinner where you will not think you were present.

But if you are with him, you will experience his warmth and generosity. And if you are really willing to put in the time, and spend a few days with him, you will experience his generosity and humanity. The devil may be in the details, but Jim is a rather handsome devil.

> "Another way would be to sit down, take a great deal of time, and read through his newsletters. They are an autobiography in astonishing detail, his newsletters. There won't be a trip you won't believe you were not on, a dinner where you will not think you were present."

John

61

Overflow crowd in corridor at the Sunday evening dinner

"... a United World Service Authority agent..."

Garry Davis

It's rare to meet and befriend someone in this world of skepticism, banality and chicanery who exudes – I'll say it – love and kindness, a critical intelligence, and essence of just plain goodness. It's almost embarrassing to try to explain it. Jim was just open spiritually, intellectually, emotionally. And he communicated it to one and all. That's rare and blissful...

(Garry Davis, in the winter of 1954, founded the United World Service Authority and started printing and issuing the first World Passport. This 16-page document was published in two languages, English and Esperanto. The passports were numbered from No. 00001. This first Passport identified him as the "World Coordinator of World Government" with a proper NY State Notary Seal stamped by the cigar stand owner in the lobby of his office building which gave it "legitimacy.")

Jim had heard about me – from his teens, he told me recently – and in the late 60's arrived in Hésinque on the French-Swiss border to find me. We became fast friends discovering in each other a common love for humanity (and the theatre) as well as personal activities to illustrate and exemplify that love. His was primarily in education; mine in political "tool designing" á la Buckminster Fuller. His help in the translations of the upgraded Passport was invaluable. Following his registration as a World Government citizen, I appointed him a United World Service Authority agent commissioned to distribute our literature, receive passport applications and distribute the filled-in passports to his worldwide "constituency."...

63

During my frequent trips to Paris…I stayed at Jim's famous "world space," Studio 2A, 83 rue de la Tombe-Issoire, a 'home-away-from-home' for literally legions of world travelers….

Then, on September 17, 1972, the French government attacked! French security agents, armed with a perquisition order signed by a Juge d'Instruction of the Tribunal de Grande Instance, Mulhouse, seized all available passports from my living-room office, and on June 22, 1973, officially charged me with "escroquerie" (swindling), and "méprise dans l'ésprit public" or "scorning the public mind," a somewhat bizarre French crime…

The French police, knowing of my connection with Jim, and searching for evidence to justify the "escroquerie" charge, interrogated him as a possible "accomplice." As a United States citizen living in France, a Paris apartment owner, teaching at an important university, and given the French visa system which permitted residency, he was placed on the legal razor's edge between expediency and idealism….

"It's almost embarrassing to try to explain it. Jim was just open spiritually, intellectually, emotionally. And he communicated it to one and all. That's rare and blissful…"

Garry

Ted Joans, Stanley Cohen and Jim, July 1995

At the Cannes Film Festival, photo by Baxter

"Just Good Fortune or Destiny"

Catherine Monnet

If I were to name one friend who enriched my life more than any other, it would probably be Jim Haynes. I'm not sure if it was just good fortune or destiny, but in either case our meeting resulted in a Paris institution, the now famous Sunday night dinners at Jim's A2 atelier.

To explain how I met Jim, I need to backtrack well over twenty years.

In 1978, I moved to Paris on a whim with the intention of spending a year while I was still young, single and adventurous. The fact that I didn't speak French and had only enough money to last two months didn't discourage me from what my parents considered a certain folly. At least I knew one person I could call when I arrived in Paris.

As soon as I landed at the airport one misty grey November afternoon, I phoned my young French Moroccan friend Claude Senouf whom I had met a few months earlier in Los Angeles. He owned a little restaurant in Venice Beach, called the "Casablanca," which I reviewed for a restaurant article commissioned by *Los Angeles Magazine*. When I mentioned some vague dream of going to live in Paris one day, Claude told me his parents owned an apartment in St. Germain and that I could stay with him the next time he was visiting Paris. This was the little spark that ignited my burning desire to move to France.

When I called Claude, waking him up at three o'clock in the afternoon, he seemed unfazed that I had taken him up on his offer and actually flew all the way to Paris. Claude told me to take a taxi and come join him at his parent's flat. When I arrived, he was on the phone making plans for the evening, discussing where and with whom he would be having dinner, as was the custom it seems.

Still on jet lag, I found myself several hours later dining at the *Coupole* in Montparnasse with a group of five or six other friends. There was a charming young woman named Colette Negrier who spoke English and noticed my total bewilderment. When I explained to her that I had come to Paris to live for a while but that I didn't know a soul in the city, she said, with a very thick French accent, "I know an American man... Jim. You must go see him. He knows everybody and maybe he can help you."

Since Claude's "visit" in Paris was just a stopover on his way to Casablanca, I was about to find myself homeless, and quickly resorted to calling Colette's friend.

"Hello, is this Jim Haynes?"

"Speaking." He answered in curt deep voice, which I found intimidating.

I began to explain that I got his phone number from a woman named Colette, and that she suggested I call and that...

He cut me off abruptly.

"Just come over."

"Oh...okay" I thought, feeling as if he was scolding me. Jim proceeded to kindly give me precise directions for getting to his atelier. "....And then you come down a pretty little cobblestone walkway with lots of trees. Go up the first short staircase on the right, knock on the door on your left and come in."

During our preliminary meeting, Jim suggested as nonchalantly as one offers a cup of coffee that I move in and stay in his guest bedroom upstairs. I gratefully accepted, not knowing that I would be sharing not only the room but also one of the two large beds on the floor with several other people. I was a little surprised though hardly shocked. Being a one-time hippy who used to hitchhike up and down the coast of California with flowers in my hair and love and peace in my heart, I felt quite "at home" at Jim's.

I think it was probably only the following day, when around lunchtime I heard Jim groan, "I'm hungry!"

I promptly offered to fix him something to eat, though being new in the house; I wasn't sure what ingredients I would find in the kitchen.

I took a look in the rather empty refrigerator, where I found some eggs, cheese, mushrooms, and some half empty jars of I can't remember what. The obvious solution was an omelette, which I whipped up with panache. Though I rarely had anyone to cook for, cooking was not only a hobby but an unexploited passion.

When it was ready, I called Jim, who had been typing away in his room.

He took a couple of bites and then moaned as though he was having an orgasm, "Oh, oh, this is the best omelette I ever ate!!"

I appreciated his enthusiasm and felt quite satisfied to be of service. Little did I know what was to follow.

Though my intention was to find work and a place to stay as quickly as possible, I must say that I was very happy living at Jim's. I was immediately impressed by his kindness, generosity and open spirit. Wayward souls of every nationality wandered in and out, chatted, drank, ate, and slept. His house key floated from one needy houseguest to another, as people showed up on his doorstep, friends of friends of friends. Being a completely trustful soul, Jim never turned anyone away. He never considered himself an American ex-patriot; he was just another human being, and a citizen of the world.

What Jim did to earn a living remained a mystery to me. Besides teaching media studies and sexual politics at the University of Paris VIII once a week, he was involved in all sorts of creative activities; writing, publishing, producing videos, organizing venues, along with leading charitable projects like sending boxes of clothes and food to Poland. Of course Jim always denied, "working" at all.

"Fullering" he called it, a word he coined to describe expending time and energy doing things one considered fulfilling.

I don't think any of Jim's "fullering" brought in huge sums of money but somehow he got by. In any case, whatever he made he shared and it seemed his generosity paid off. Besides hundreds of friends I saw a surprising number of lovely young ladies who repaid Jim's kindness with kisses, cuddles and when Jim was lucky, a warm body to share his bed for a night, a week and sometimes much longer.

I too was grateful for Jim's hospitality and since I wasn't yet making enough money to contribute to the household, the least I could do was to "fuller," acting as the resident cook. Not only did I enjoy having guests to cook for, but everyone who was living at Jim's, passing through, or just staying for dinner enjoyed eating what I cooked. The more cooking I did, the more guests we collected.

It soon became evident to me that Jim's modest income could not continue to feed all these wonderful guests. What to do?

I can't remember if it was my suggestion or if Jim and I came to a mutual conclusion, but it seemed the best solution was to organize evening meals a couple of times a week and to ask for a "contribution" from guests. Jim, true to his generous nature, proposed to pay me 100 francs for preparing each meal.

We scheduled the dinners for Wednesday and Saturday night and I quickly wrote up a month's worth of menus that Jim photocopied and handed out to anyone who came to visit. Everyone found it a great idea. Jim knew so many people that each dinner honoured the birthday of at least three or four of his friends. (Whenever Jim met someone new, one of the first bits of information he asked, besides sexual preferences, was their birth date.)

In the beginning there were only about twenty guests for dinner, and we all sat crowded together around Jim's long kitchen table. However, these sit down dinners lasted only a few weeks since there were soon too many guests to accommodate sitting down. So, we began to serve the dinner buffet style, obliging our guests to eat standing up, plate in hand. This delighted Jim who not only hated sitting around a table but also loved the idea that everyone could move about and mingle.

As the dinner format changed, so did my meals. No more meats that had to be cut with a knife and fork, no more complicated dishes and no more pretty presentations on the plate. We had to purchase restaurant equipment such as enormous mixing bowls, extra large baking pans and ten–gallon pots, to prepare and serve up the growing quantities of food. Fortunately, Jim had a large professional stove with a double oven in which we could pile up to ten baking sheets or pie pans at once, and keep enough food hot to serve one hundred at a time.

These dinners became increasingly difficult to prepare alone. It became the custom that whoever was staying at Jim's helped out, cutting, chopping or stirring. Whenever someone came over for a coffee and a chat, they also found themselves chopping up three kilos of onions, peeling five kilos of apples or beating up four litres of whipped cream. Making the meal became a social activity to be shared with a multitude of friends; a perfect communal enterprise.

After about six months, I finally found some work teaching ballet five days a week and could afford to pay for my own apartment. I reluctantly moved out of Jim's. He would have been happy to keep me as a permanent resident, but I felt there were more needy guests than I, and being less tolerant than Jim, I yearned for my own space.

Since I was less available to cook, we shifted from the schedule of twice a week, to Sunday evening only, my day off. This turned out to be the ideal night, since most people are busy during the week, tired from rising early and working, and they usually have something else going Friday or Saturday nights. And in France, shopping on Sunday is still limited to a few little "épiceries" providing you with the essentials, but seldom enough to make a good meal.

The Sunday dinners were officially born.

As time went on, I became less available to cook even on

Sunday. Meeting my husband and starting a family curtailed my availability drastically. Jack Moore, a long time friend who lived at Jim's, became the major Sunday night chef for many years. He also loved to cook and earned a great reputation for turning out tons of hearty, tasty dishes to please the ever-growing crowds. When neither Jack nor I were available, Jim was able to find "guest chefs", friends or visitors who were brave enough, and ambitious enough to tackle a three-course dinner for anywhere from fifty to one hundred guests. Sometimes, even if I couldn't cook the whole meal, I would come back from time to time, and prepare a dessert, Jim's favourite part of the meal.

I always did and still do take great pleasure cooking at Jim's, who is always there to do the shopping and help out between all those weekend phone calls when people ring to book for dinner. He's become an excellent vegetable chopper, can opener, and helps me heave around those enormous pots of chile, stew or pasta. He often breaks into song, an air or two from some antiquated musical comedy that he and I can appreciate, if no one else.

These dinners have been going on almost uninterrupted for twenty-six years. (Jim always takes a three-week hiatus in August for the Festival in Edinburgh). They have been written up countless times in newspapers of every nationality, flight magazines, and newsletters. And though Jim has never advertised, his home is continually booked every Sunday night simply from word of mouth. There are many "regulars" who have come faithfully almost every Sunday over the years, and there are always new people too.

The reason the dinners are so successful has little to do with the food, (which is usually quite good by the way) and everything to do with the host. I think the fact that everyone is crowded in the kitchen-salon of a fifty square meter atelier adds to the charm. You can't help but rub and knock elbows with your neighbour, and Jim makes sure that everyone, once being introduced, keeps talking. He sits perched on a stool as the meal is served, shouting out the names on his guest list and reminding everyone that they are not only there to eat but to talk to one another. It is the perfect place to meet, to network, and to fall in love. Jim has no idea how many romances have bloomed, or long time friendships have been established among people attending his dinners.

My gratitude towards Jim extends far beyond the Sunday dinners. Jim made it possible for me to live in Paris long enough to become self-sustaining. His generosity changed the whole course of my life, since I never would have been able to make a career in dancing, (he also helped me organize two trips to perform at the Edinburgh Festival), I never would have met my American flatmate (at Jim's) who introduced me to my husband with whom I have two beautiful children, and the whole chain of events resulting in a fulfilled life in Paris would never have occurred if it weren't for Jim.

I really do love Jim. And though love is best left unexplained, I can clearly define one reason why I appreciate him. It's because "he is who he is." There are no masks, no frills, no put-ons, no complexes, no attempts to influence, impress, manipulate, simulate or whatever else most human beings spend so much time doing. Most of the time he's truly sweet, generous and kind, but every once in a while he can be a bit of a grouch or a grump, just to remind us he's human. But in any case, he's always authentically Jim.

"I can clearly define one reason why I appreciate him. It's because "he is who he is." There are no masks, no frills, no put-ons, no complexes, no attempts to influence, impress, manipulate, simulate or whatever else most human beings spend so much time doing."

Catherine

Antonia Hoogewerf and Jim in the Fairlawn Hotel garden in Calcutta,
February 2005

"The Sunday Night Salon...
or the Night I Met Jim Haynes"

Antonia Hoogewerf

I met Jim one May evening at a Gala of Vernissages by the *Café La Palette* in the rue de Seine. Little did I know that I would soon be embroiled in a different world, a small atelier in a leafy alley in the 14th arrondissement where painters and writers and musicians and travellers and people who just wander in, come to have dinner with Jim of a Sunday night.

I had recently moved to Paris, maybe the most romantic liberal and civilised city in the world, the epitomy of culture and beauty, and Jim shares this love of Paris. He is a city person through and through, people are his life's blood. We never go out together but we pick up people – at the cinema, on the Metro, in buses, in restaurants, and someone gets handed an invitation to Dinner. In Jim I recognised at once a spirit which had not come into my orbit before but was instantly complementary to everything I think – and far removed from the life I had always lived. What was it Noel Coward said about the "English upper middle classes"? Not very complimentary, but that was my world – Hunt Balls, shooting, polo, sailing at Cowes, racing at Ascot, children dogs and horses, and then La France Profonde. All a far cry from the world of Jim Haynes, yet I immediately felt at home with him.

He has a great reputation which sails before him (unknown to me then!) but this man is the complete gentleman, loving the sweet things of life and relentless in his pursuit of them. And his manners are perfect. He hates violence, abuse and excess of any kind. He is discreet, open-hearted and generous to a fault (literally, sometimes).

I never knew him in the old days, let alone the sixties and when I say I wish I had, he says in his gravelly Louisiana accents: "Honey, you couldn't have kept up with me!" Which is probably true. He is a life-enhancer with true compassion and love for his fellows, and one of the few people I know who sincerely wishes the happiness and freedom of every human being, recognising both their equality and their uniqueness.

The Sunday Night Dinners started in the late seventies and soon became a favourite haunt of the Paris cognoscenti, a "last bastion of the Paris underground". Shortly after we met, Jim's main cook left and suddenly he had a hundred people coming to dinner and no cook. I had often catered for large parties so I offered to help. Jim was clearly scared I could not do it! (I guess I don't look very practical.) Then one Sunday he let me try out an Indian dinner on his guests, which luckily worked out pretty well and we were away.

I like to cook on a Saturday afternoon. The thing that gets you at first is the quantities required and the time it takes. And it's never enough for Jim. If you suggest 6 kilos he will say 8, if you say 10 he will say 12. Anyone around is roped in to help with the vegetables, but Jim and I work steadily – well mostly me! – in the calm light of the lofty-windowed Atelier, between strolling out to shop for extra or forgotten items and then having supper together. A pleasant and laid-back way to spend a Saturday.

Then on Sunday I turn up to oversee last minute things and heat up the main dishes. Someone chops the bread and Seamus arrives to cook the rice. Jim takes on a different persona on Sunday evenings. Up to seven o'clock he is his normal amiable self, ambling round the kitchen, answering the phone, taking out garbage, giving hugs to those in need, chopping up onions (a job no-one else likes doing) and generally trying to be useful. Suddenly he galvanises into a holy terror, barking orders left and right as the magic hour of eight draws near. "Zero hour minus thirty!" he yells, "Zero hour minus ten!" If people arrive early they are told "Go away! We're not ready!" Then at eight o'clock precisely the doors open and the hordes pour into the little Atelier.

No-one is allowed to sit in a corner. "Talk! Why aren't you talking? Sally this is Paul, Paul Sylvia, Sylvia John, come on, talk!" Jim sits on his stool wearing a large apron, introducing everyone to each other, often people he has never met before, and a lot that he has. He has a prodigious memory for names and faces and an incredible address book. There are seven or eight faithfuls who come every Sunday, but the majority are new people who have heard about it from newspapers and magazines or who are brought along by friends.

Here on a Sunday evening in Paris, romance blossoms, love affairs are begun and ended, jobs, work, commissions sought, lost and found, friendships formed and broken. Dance, theatre, cinema, writing, painting, poetry, photography are all avidly discussed. Everyone feels caught up in the excited hubbub of things happening. It is a great exchange of humanity, ideas, philosophy and the art of life. The fact is, people want to meet people and none more so than Jim Haynes. Putting people in touch with each other is what makes him tick, and he does it with absolute generosity. Around eleven o'clock he starts shooing everyone out. "Jim's tired! Jim wants to go to bed! Good night!" and they leave, having enjoyed a stimulating evening of good (we hope) food and great and varied company. Jim is a man who changes and enriches people's lives and who changed and enriched my life. Thank you sweetheart for being there.

"Talk! Why aren't you talking? Sally this is Paul, Paul Sylvia, Sylvia John, come on, talk!'

Jim sits on his stool wearing a large apron and directing operations, introducing everyone to each other, often people he has never met before, and a lot that he has. He has a prodigious memory for names and faces and an incredible address book."

Antonia

Another Sunday evening dinner at A2

"A one-man United Nations at dinner"

Julia Watson

PARIS, July 20 (UPI) -- Jim Haynes is a one-man embodiment of the spirit of the United Nations. The self-proclaimed peace-seeking leaders of the world could learn a thing or four from this genial man. How to bring people from different backgrounds happily together would be one. It's easy: You feed them supper in Paris on a Sunday.

An expat American from Louisiana since military service in the U.S. Air Force sent him to Scotland near Edinburgh in 1956, Haynes has been based in Paris for more than 25 years. Many of those years have been spent as a professor of sexual studies at the University of Vincennes. But though that may seem an odd discipline to some, this is not what he is primarily known for among his friends -- of which there are scores. Across the world, hundreds of people can talk about Haynes, his kindness and generosity from the first-hand experience of having attended one of his regular Sunday dinner parties. More than 100,000 such people so far, in fact. And most of them complete strangers to him.

In the early days you might have been squeezed into his 14th arrondissement atelier next to John Lennon or Indira Gandhi. These days, the 50 or more people who show up for a simple but hearty three-course meal, cooked by a changing run of friends and with all the wine and beer you can drink, are likely to be less familiar. And certainly so to one another. They've come because somewhere on their travels someone has said, "If you're in Paris on a Sunday, you should go and eat at Jim's."

Begun when a ballet dancer from Los Angeles who had taken shelter at his book-and-video-lined studio wanted to repay his hospitality by cooking a gourmet meal for his friends, the suppers became a regular fixture. And grew in size.

Eventually, Haynes was forced to ask his guests for contributions toward the food. But there's nowhere in Paris where you can eat a meal to pack your stomach full with limitless wine and beer for about $20. And nowhere else to find yourself so easily in the contented company of world travelers and Parisians.

And Haynes makes sure you are indeed put in touch with your fellow diners. He may not have met them before himself, but he will be able to name every one of them and introduce them by country, occupation or interest.

This is a man whose many address books are grouped by nation. Borders and boundaries mean little to him. At one point he carried a Citizen of the World Passport devised with a friend, which contained a photograph, the usual physical descriptives and a postage stamp. A number of baffled immigration officers nevertheless accepted it as valid. In the Soviet Union during the 1980s when permits were necessary for Russians to travel, he arrived in Moscow with a gaggle of girls from Leningrad he had managed to smuggle onto the train. And successfully smuggled back again.

His autobiography, *Thanks for Coming!* (Faber & Faber) has probably the longest acknowledgments section ever published, running to several pages. It's a census of many of the key figures of the 1960s as well as ordinary Jacks and Jills. He works hard to keep in touch with all of them.

Many will have met him after he left the Air Force, through the paperback bookshop he opened in Edinburgh, or the Traverse Theatre he launched there, or maybe wandering the annual Edinburgh Festival of which he has long been a cornerstone. If not, they might have stumbled upon him in London in the '60s at the "Arts Lab" he began in Drury Lane, an avant-garde space for experimental theatre, film and exhibitions that was an essential meeting place. Or perhaps through the underground magazine *Suck* he launched with Germaine Greer.

An entirely benign spirit, he is good at taking a provocative and sometimes oblique approach to making a point over an issue about which he is passionate. In 1968, when London was erupting in demonstrations against American involvement in Vietnam, he and black comedian Dick Gregory worked on a "Dick Gregory for President" campaign, possibly the only two people on it. Gregory wore denim overalls and an untrimmed, full beard. This presentation was the crucial strut of their platform: If U.S. men could be persuaded, their theory went, not to shave nor wear anything but overalls, the barbers and tailors of the United States would feel the loss of income so strongly they would agree to vote against the war. London high society in all its satin finery was captivated. The pair were invited all over town to make their case.

These days, when Jim Haynes is not on one of his many trips to friends across the globe, it is on his doorstep that the world shows up. According to Natalia Antelava, a journalist from the Republic of Georgia, "It was the high point of our trip to Paris."

To dine "chez Jim," call 0033.143271767, or (in Paris) 0143271767.

"Across the world, hundreds of people can talk about Haynes, his kindness and generosity from the first-hand experience of having attended one of his regular Sunday dinner parties. More than 100,000 such people so far, in fact. And most of them complete strangers to him."

Julia

Karolina Blåberg and Jim in a rickshaw in Calcutta, February 2005, photo by Antonia Hoogewerf

"Jim is my guru, I just follow him!"

Karolina Blåberg

That was my joyful and somewhat careless answer to a Canadien literary agent in Delhi last February. She was curious to learn about my raison d'être with Jim in India at a Shakespearien theatre opening. I might have told her just as well the official theme of our journey: to celebrate life! What else could it be, on the road with James Haynes!

The scene off stage that night was even more dramatic since it was Jim's departure after a fortnight of our magical mystery tour in India. And to give more colour to our goodbyes we threw some flower petals over this world citizen together with our Delhi friend Sanjeev Prakash, who came to know Jim in the early 70's. Needless to say that Jim's embarrassment was huge, how could he handle being treated as an idol, or a guru, even in India ?

Little did I know about how my first encounter with Jim Haynes would affect my life, that one day I would find myself in India with him. It happened in 1989 in Finland, the country where I was born. I had been contracted to join the Lahti International Writer's Reunion, a major literary event in the remote country of the thousand lakes. The happening, that later became bi-annual, began in the early 60's during the cold war at its coldest. Finnish publishers, such as Erkki Reenpää from the Otava publishing house and other concerned intellectuals wanted to create a meeting in order to facilitate a dialogue between the east and the west. And also to show foreign writers in flesh and blood to the highly curious and quite private Finnish readers. As we know the ambitious literary figures privilege Stockholm, if ever they travel to the dark north, not knowing that excessive exposure is harmful in the Lutheran world and irritates the Nobel jury...

In the early 60's Eastern and Soviet writers had very limited opportunities to exchange ideas or travel. As the Estonian writer, Tallinn based Jaan Kross puts it, his only foreign travelling was to Finland. And he remembers well, coming back to the Tallinn harbour together with his wife, the precious Western books given to them in Finland had to be thrown to the Baltic sea before entering the iron curtain. Finland had a very peculiar geopolitical situation those days. Maybe only history will tell, and the sealed archives, what was really going on between Moscow and Helsinki. The Finns lived a full Western democratic life, with the powerful knowledge of the nearness of the "big bear", as the neighbor was called. But somehow the menace is inbuilt in Finnish genetics. Our colonial past has left traces, eight centuries under Swedish domination and one by Tsars ruling from St. Petersburg. up to our declaration of independence in 1917, and the fragile start of a new nation where for a long time nothing could be taken for granted.

At the Lahti reunion, the selection of the Eastern delegates was carefully done by Moscou, made up of writers in heavy overcoats, translators and party officials. But nevertheless, some exchange of ideas was possible under the hectic midsummer sun, white nights, sauna and vodka. The meeting was always held just round about the summer solstice, late June, outdoors in a beautiful manor park under ancient oak trees. The image of Lahti is people sitting all over on the lawn in small groups with their earphones, a scene where Jim Haynes can be pictured, all far away from stuffy congress venues or intellectual pretending even though many of the brightest thinkers of our times had joined the gathering. The essence of it all was to talk, celebrate life and make long-term friendships. And for many, the best moment was the midnight football match, Finland against the rest of the world, heartbreakingly regretted by Salman Rushdie.

One of the participants at the very first Lahti meeting was the Cuban poet Pablo Armando Fernández . *Il n'y a pas de hasard*. He had been contacted earlier in London by Erkki Reenpää, the great aficionado of South American writing and the Hispanic world. He had put together an anthology of South American poetry including Pablo's work and more than naturally Pablo was invited to join the first reunion. After all his travelling ever since, Pablo still recalls the magic of those white nights.

Curiously enough Jim and I were brought together by Cuba as well. We had met briefly in Helsinki already at the Pen Club cocktail, hosted by the WSOY publishing house, the social and media opening of the meeting. Jim had made his usual speedy presentation for me, including his youth in Venezuela and his restaurant in Paris. My role in the meeting was to take care of the Hispanic minority, since that year the budget didn't allow us simultaneous translation into Spanish. Once we had reached Lahti, 100 kms. from Helsinki, my responsibilities started to take shape. A Cuban writer, Stockholm based Réné Vázquez Díaz was one of the key note speakers on the opening panel and, of course, he had written his speech only in Spanish. As an act of good will towards the translators and the press, it had to be reborn in English in no time. My bright idea was to catch Jim together with Réné and his paper, have them seated on a bench in the park and start taking notes. I must admit I don't remember if the paper ever saw the light in English or not. But we had a great moment of joy and sharing on that bench. The scene was brought back to my mind at the end of March when Réné was in Paris promoting his latest book, *Florina*, the first part of his erotic trilogy.

Jim and Finland have a long history that started way back in Lousiana, where his neighbor was a Finnish lady who charmed the young boy with her pies. Jim's first real landing on Finnish soil was in Turku in the 60's when he came over invited to inspect theatre plays. He arrived in December and slipped on his behind the minute he got off the plane, of course the airport was under ice. Later in Turku he ended up in a fight when a jealous husband attacked him after being too friendly with the poor man's wife, a beautiful actress. And even more ice was on the way out. Jim took the overnight ferry from Turku to Stockholm praying the whole way that it wouldn't break. Even titanic Hollywood special effects sound weak in comparison with the icebreaking boats in the Baltic winter. All this didn't discourage Jim when he heard about this casual literary meeting in Lahti and decided to join in 1985. He found out about it from two charming Finnish girls he happened to meet in his quartier in Paris and invite over for a cup of tea.

By the time we met at the Lahti meeting, he was already a great connaisseur of the Finnish literary and human scene and had made many Finnish friends. Jim kept coming back to Lahti until 1999 combining it with activities either/or both in Scandinavia and the East. With the passing of years, Jim's popularity in Finland only increased, and he became a true godfather of the meeting. His modesty for drinking made him a kind of collective memory of the white nights. And his many qualities were appreciated, his kindness, diplomacy and huge experience with life and living. I even remember him reciting his sharp poetry in an open mike evening!

Very recently, Jim returned from Barcelona, where he had met among others Jaume Subirana, a Catalan poet he first met in Lahti in 1999. Finnish intellectuals know their way to Jim's dinners where they appreciate the informal ambience and the generous bar. Lahti is still a living connection among so many in Jim's huge network.

It has now been seven years since I have a home in Montparnasse, which I discovered at the age of 18, and where I secretly decided to come back to stay one day. It is a privilege to share this corner of Paris with Jim, the *Rosebud, le Select* and *la Coupole*, hélas not what it used to be as Jim sighs with regret. And our joyful escapades on the Right Bank, mainly to the Terminus Nord, to welcome John Calder from London with champagne and oysters, after his odyssean Eurostar.

The Lahti international writers reunion is not just a separate happening, it is a voyage that goes on every two years, as the co-chairman of the meeting, a Finnish philosopher Tuomas Nevan-linna puts it. Continuity is certainly one of Jim's qualities, as many of his old friends know.

"Lahti, the name sounds like a tasty Eastern European dish with lots of garlic," was Jim's off the record comment once. It makes sense, since the restaurant named *Garlic* is his favourite in Helsinki, garlic being one of the true values in the Haynesian world.

Tim Steffa, Jim's American friend in Helsinki, gave his voice to a Nokia commercial that all of you have heard. In a simple way it reflects Jim's basic operations too, it goes:
Nokia, connecting people.

"It is a privilege to share this corner of Paris with Jim, the Rosebud, le Select and la Coupole, hélas not what it used to be as Jim sighs with regret. And our joyful escapades on the Right Bank, mainly to the Terminus Nord, to welcome John Calder from London with champagne and oysters, after his odyssean Eurostar."

Karolina

A guest arrives...another Sunday evening chez Jim (Séamas McSwiney serves a salad; Roger Ward waits for his name to be checked.)

"Dinner in Paris — But For Seventy!"

Marion Winik

Robb pulls a tortilla out of the frying pan and slaps it on the baking sheet; I trowel on a layer of spinach and mushrooms and cover it with sliced gruyere. He piles on another tortilla; I add a second story of fragrant mortar. He follows instantly with the third and final tortilla, which I sprinkle with a bit more cheese. My hand has barely moved out of range when he moves back in with the ladle, drizzling the rich smoked chile sauce over the stack.

"This batch is ready to bake," he pronounces, bending to peek into the oven. "Pull the first ones out and start serving."

Thank God, I'm thinking, because these people are definitely hungry. The guacamole, ceviche, and salsa bowls have been licked clean, and clusters of eager diners are now camped out at the serving table, making eyes at the beans and rice. Meanwhile, snippets of a dozen conversations ricochet around us — politics in Berlin, golf in South America, is there such a thing as grunge poetry, have you seen the new Bertolucci, were you here last week when they served that amazing lamb? And those are only the ones in the languages I understand. God knows what those excitable Italians are on about. Yet even they are silenced by the sight of me turning from the oven with a steaming tray of enchiladas in my oven-mitted hand.

You know, when you picture a weekend in Paris with your sweetheart, certain images come to mind. The Seine, for example. The Champs-Elysées. A moonlit walk at the Eiffel Tower. Two glasses of Kir Royale at a sidewalk café. One of the things that doesn't occur to you right off is that you'll be devoting your weekend to cooking dinner for seventy strangers in a tiny apartment near the southern city limits. And yet that is exactly what happened to my boyfriend Robb and me once we fell under the sway of Jim Haynes, a character in whom the spirits of Tom Sawyer, Andy Warhol, and Mother Teresa unite.

For the past twenty-seven years, the expatriate Haynes has given a Sunday night dinner party at his flat in the 14th arrondissement. And has welcomed any and all who come to dine. Yes, really — you just call to say you're coming, you bring a donation if you can afford it, you show up at 7:30, and you're one of the gang. I first heard about Haynes's soirées when asking for Paris tips from a well-travelled friend in Texas. "It sounds kind of weird," I commented to her. "Why would someone give a dinner for a bunch of strangers? And who would want to go to a big dinner party where they don't even know anybody?"

"Oh, you'll know somebody. Somebody who knows somebody you know. Or someone who lives in the village in Latvia your great-grandparents emigrated from. If most people in the world exist at six degrees of separation, Jim Haynes's party cuts it down to two or three."

I was intrigued, and tucked Haynes's number into my guidebook.

We arrive in Paris on a Saturday morning and check into a hotel not far from Haynes's apartment in the Alésia section of town — south of Montparnasse, a relaxed residential area inhabited by professors and professionals, writers and families, perhaps the Paris equivalent of Manhattan's Upper West Side. "Let's see if we can drop in and visit the guy," I suggest to Robb. "Then we can decide if we really want to go tomorrow night."

Having agreed to a visit, Haynes is waiting on the stoop when we arrive, completely disheveled. (Over the course of the weekend, I am to learn that Haynes is always completely disheveled, except when he gets dressed up. Then he's only somewhat disheveled.) At 62, his collar-length shock of dark hair has less gray than you might expect. It is strange hair, almost wig-like in its thickness and the odd angle at which it sprouts from his head, several pieces making a hard right turn at the place where the earpiece of his glasses would be if he were wearing them. His eyes are a bright, deep brown full of wit and understanding, and bear the evidence of a lifetime of smiles. His moustache, like his hair, wears him. He looks like a mad scientist, a crazy artist, a nutty professor. He is wearing a half-buttoned shirt and boxer shorts and holding a cup of coffee. "Marion and Robb!" he calls, and ushers us in.

When you first see Haynes's shoebox apartment – on the first floor, right off the foyer of the building, the front door opens onto a kitchen which is the only room on the main floor, with some loft bedrooms perched above it and a basement below – you cannot imagine giving a dinner party for seven here, much less seventy. I assume there must be some other space, some Grand Salon in which the event will occur.

Over coffee, I coax out of him the broad outlines of his background. Born in Shreveport, Louisiana, he spent part of his childhood in Venezuela and part in an all-boy military school. Upon matriculation at Louisiana State University in Baton Rouge, he began forthwith to make up for the deprivations of the military school years. "I majored in chasing women, gambling, and drinking," he says. "They called it economics, I think." At 20, he joined the Air Force and was sent to Scotland. He has not lived in the United States since.

During the 50's and 60's, Haynes was a primary mover and shaker of alternative culture in both Edinburgh and London. He owned a bookshop, ran a theater, and founded the Arts Lab, a sixties performance space/be-in/crash pad which was the model for offspring all over the world, most famously the Milky Way in Amsterdam. In 1969, he received a call from the University of Paris, asking if he could come teach a seminar. Having neither professorial credentials nor a word of French language, he was a bit surprised. But the University had assured him he was what they wanted. The student riots in Paris the preceding year had germinated from com-

91

plaints about the rigidity and classicism of the university curriculum. The administration saw Haynes's way-out course on Media and The Creative Process as be a bone to throw the angry students. A bone with plenty of meat on it — almost twenty years later, Haynes is still teaching that course and others.

The dinners began back shortly after his arrival in the city, as a means of raising money to print the first book issued by his homegrown publishing venture, Handshake Press. Once the money was raised, the diners refused to stop coming. With no major interruptions since that time, the tradition has continued; today any profits go to relief efforts in Eastern Europe.

"So do you cook this dinner yourself?" Robb asks, turning the conversation to the subject always foremost on his mind.

"Well, normally it's my friend Jack, with whom I trade room and board for culinary services. But sorry to say, Jack's out of town and I'm afraid I can't guarantee anything. My old girlfriend Corinne is supposed to cook a pasta del mare, but I don't have the ingredients for her yet and —"

"Too bad I didn't know," says Robb casually. "I would have cooked."

"Yeah, too bad," I chime in. "You know, Robb's a food writer and a really great chef. He writes cookbooks!"

"Well," Jim replies cannily, "it's never too late."

Robb is not going to get out of this one. After ten minutes of hemming and hawing, he realizes that Jim has an answer to every objection, including sources for the exotic ingredients he'll need for a gourmet adaptation of Tex-Mex enchiladas. He gives up, and is immediately whisked into a whirlwind of shopping. This is accomplished in numerous short forays on foot, by metro and by bus, bringing back only as much on each trip as can be carried. Meanwhile, someone must remain at the apartment at all times to answer the phone and take reservations for tomorrow night.

To assist in these projects, Jim introduces two of the current boarders at what I'm coming to think of as the Jim Haynes Foundation for World Friendship and Home for Wayward Boys and

Girls. There's Katya, a tall, slender aspiring jazz singer from Saint Petersburg — possibly his current girlfriend —and Jerome, a French country boy in the big city, a cross between a puppy dog and a club kid, whose life now consists of discos and "Zheem's" dinners. Jerome is sent out with the dolly to a supermarket nearby to load up on staples; Katya is assigned to wait by the phone until Jim and Robb get back from the fishmarket and we start prepping ceviche.

In the course of this afternoon, I get to know Haynes both from his anecdotes and from clues found in his apartment. There's his autobiography, *Thanks for Coming*, which is dedicated to a list of people nineteen pages in length and includes a cast of characters ranging from R. Crumb to Jean Shrimpton. There's his *People to People* series of guides to Eastern Europe, which contain the names and addresses of people in those countries who would be pleased to welcome travelers into their homes. There is an awesome collection of movies on tape in the basement. And there are Jim's stories, which usually begin with a chance encounter on the street or in a restaurant and end several continents, love affairs, art projects and business ventures later with a line like, "... and that's where I got this stove."

We chop and shred late into the night, joined by a young girl named Sam from Germany and a student of Jim's from the university who needs a recommendation for study abroad. Finally, we've done all we can. When we depart, the girls are drinking wine and watching French MTV, Jerome is teaching Katya the words to "La Vie En Rose," and Jim, who neither drinks nor smokes, is playing an impressive-looking game of two-deck solitaire.

"A houseguest from Poland inflicted this game on me," he explains, "and I've never been the same since."

When we arrive at noon on Sunday, Jim is waiting by the phone like a teenager. "Bookings are low," he complains. "Where is everybody? It looks like we may have no more than forty people tonight."

"Forty would be fine," Robb says, but clearly Jim doesn't think so. He thinks about sixty or seventy is perfect. I still can't imagine where he's going to put any of these people.

93

At 6 pm, the transformation of the apartment begins. The front door is opened wide, and the foyer outside becomes the bar, an old breakfront under the staircase stocked with wine, juice, ice and plastic glasses. Inside the kitchen, all the furniture except for the table and one long, low couch is wheeled back into the laundry room. ("This was one of Jerome's great ideas," Jim explains. "After a couple of months of hauling the television and stereo around, he put everything on wheels.") The table slides to the end of the room, closing off a workspace by the stove. And the front wall of the room, former site of the television and shelves, is revealed to be a series of French doors, now thrown open to the stoop and alley (Jim calls it "the garden") beyond.

"Now you see," says Jim. "We can have as many as ninety!"

Yeah, I'm thinking, as long as it doesn't rain.

The enchiladas come out of the oven, we top them with sour cream and thinly-sliced Moroccan peppers - the closest thing we could get to jalapenos - and pass them into waiting hands. As soon as there's a pause in the action, Jim takes a break from his incessant chanting of introductions — "Rico, this is Liesl, Edi, Viveka, Hans, Michael, Kitty, Siobahn, Robb, Marion, and you know Ted and Myra, don't you? from the bookshop?" — grabs two plates and motions me to follow him. We climb the stairs to the second floor of the building.

"It's for my neighbor," he explains.

His knock is answered by an ancient Parisian lady and her tiny pooch. "Bonsoir, Zheem," she says with a grande dame smile. He offers the plates in halting but courtly French; a younger man emerges from the dust motes behind her to receive them.

"It's her son," Jim explains after we bid them goodnight. "He takes care of her."

And Jim Haynes takes care of both of them, and anyone else who crosses his path. Picking my way downstairs behind him through the diners seated on the steps, I feel a rush of affection for this odd but unmistakable gentleman, for the kindness and love of people that are the motive force behind his unusual life.

"...the most tolerant person I know - he is a magician - he changes people's life..."

Susi Wyss

Guess why I am the happiest girl in town? Because I am the very lucky neighbor of Jim. The one and only Jimmy-Boy! Jim as you know - is unique. He is the most helpful tolerant person I know - he is a magician - he changes people's life - he embellishes his "entourage" he makes things happen, he is a truly generous mensch. He is my banker, my confident, my friend. He is simply a delicious guy. He couldn't cook an egg many years ago, now he often cooks himself for 60 to 100 people on his famous Sunday Dinners. Oh yes - he is the greatest host, my cuddily grizzly Bear, younger than anyone else at heart. I love you Jim, long live Jim! Thank you for being here. Jim forever, forever Jim. Your fervent fan and admirer, Susi-Q

Incontrarsi

TESTO E FOTO
DI JOHN BRUNTON

Jim Haynes (a lato) è uno statunitense in Europa dal 1969. Ogni domenica sera, nella sua piccola casa di rue de la Tombe Issoire (sotto), ospita a cena dalle 50 alle 100 persone.

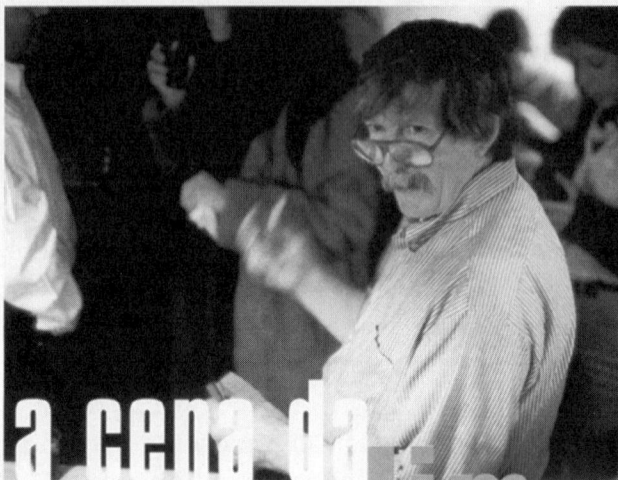

Tutti a cena da Jim

Dove si può incontrare un monaco buddhista che conversa con un diplomatico cubano o un editore di libri new age che scambia opinioni con una casalinga francese?

A **Parigi**
naturalmente, dove una persona molto speciale, ogni domenica, apre la sua casa per cena

La chiave che spalanca la porta a uno dei segreti meglio conservati e più piacevoli di Parigi ha otto cifre. È il numero di telefono di Jim Haynes, americano naturalizzato in Europa dal 1969. Telefonategli in qualsiasi momento e lui vi inviterà a cena: infatti Jim, da oltre trent'anni, ogni domenica apre la sua casa a tutti quelli che desiderano trascorrere una serata in compagnia di persone provenienti >

Panorama Travel Magazine, Italian edition, a Jim Haynes special, February 2000

98

The way it was...the way it is...

Jim Haynes

1933: Mother rushes from Texas where she and my father are living to her mother's home in Haynesville, Louisiana for my birth, the 10th of November. Five months later we move to Shreveport where I am to live the first twelve years of my life. A quiet middle class neighborhood, 1614 Magnolia Street. A letter written to me from my mother in the early 1980s reports: "You were born at 6am at Mama's house on an early Friday morning. Actually at 6am. To all of us a very beautiful baby. There was much excitement at that house all day for Herbert (my mother's brother) was playing football against Byrd High, Shreveport that p.m. And Ve (my mother sister). Ve was having a church wedding at 8 p.m. that night. After the wedding, Albert (my father's brother) and Max (my mother's baby brother) went O'possum hunting that nite. All in all a very exciting day. ..Dad went to work in Shreveport shortly after you were born and you and I stayed on with Mama until you were five months old."

1934: Neighbor family is Greek. They have two daughters, Bessie and Mary Cocos. They teach me some naughty words in Greek. My father has a job with the Arkansas Oil and Gas Company.

1935: Listen to the radio a lot, especially at night. Favorite program: I Love a Mystery. Very scary.

1936: Play with the neighbors. Two brothers, George and Gene Newton, are good friends. Later attend L.S.U. with George. Gene becomes a football player for Tulane University.

99

1937: My mother has a job in a local women's shop that is run by her cousin. I am alone a lot and this pleases me. Spend a great deal of time bird-watching. Join the John James Audubon Society. Wander the neighborhood and make friends with the neighbors and local shop-keepers. Steal a comic book from a drug store, take it home and read it. Feel ashamed and take it back to the store. Never steal again.

1938: My mother's letter: "After you started to school (Alexandria Grammar) you joined the Cub Scouts and I was Den Mother for two years."

1939: Mother continues: "You joined the Boy Scouts and was a darn good one. ...When you were 6 years old you didn't get to start school as your birthday was in November so you went to stay with Mama as she was alone. Also do you recall the summer you and Pete (Neilson) and Ben (Crocker) went to Grandmother Haynes and you three started a bird sanctuary?"

1940: Attend Alexandria Grammar, a short walk from home. My favorite neighbors are John and Marion Daly. He is Irish and is an engraver with the local newspaper, *The Shreveport Times*. His wife, Marion, is Finnish and she spoils me with wonderful pies and cakes and tales of life in Finland. They have a son, Bill, who is older than me and a daughter, Joan, who is about my age. Joan and I play the classic games "Doctor and Nurse", "Post Office", "Spin the Bottle" and other games that involve exploring each other's bodies. Marion plants a love and a curiosity for and about Finland that sparks a life-long love of that country.

1941: Remember hearing Franklin D. Roosevelt radio address to the nation that Pearl Harbor has been bombed and the United States is at war with Japan. Mother continues: "War started and you had your little soldier uniform and was ringleader in our neighborhood on Magnolia Street. Your friends were the Greek girls, Julius

(Chapman) the Jewish boy and many others..." Do my best for the war efforts by collecting scrap metal. Mother and Father entertain service men in our home. The biggest air base in America, Barksdale, is just outside Shreveport. One man, Jean Dacquin, who is training with the Free French Air Force at Barksdale, is more or less adopted by my family and it is the first time for me to hear about France. My family stays in contact with him for the rest of their lives. The first time they travel to Europe, we visit Jean in the East of France.

1942: Organize the local kids and we play sexual exploration games in a small wooded area behind my house. Become "a chocoholic" by sneak-drinking Hersey's Chocolate straight from the can. Break out in a strange rash. Later confess to my mother's good friend and the family doctor, Dr. Margaret Akin. Also break a lot of bones.

1943: Follow the war, read *The Shreveport Times* newspaper, listen to the radio, read late at night under the covers with a flash light. Explore the neighborhood. Attend school. Catherine Hooper, my first girlfriend, and I are the two top students. Later Catherine is killed in a tragic car accident.

1944: Discover Dorothy Parker and Langston Hughes in my father's library. These two poets become major influences. The Langston Hughes poem, *I, Too, Sing America*, creates a humanist consciousness that means I will never be a racist. Dorothy Parker's influence is more subtle, but equally important. Edit a small private newspaper entitled *The Treetop News*. Circulation: one copy per issue. My father gives me some advice that I have always attempted to heed: "When you do something nice for someone, forget it immediately; when someone does something nice for you, never forget it..."

1945: The bombing of Nagasaki and Hiroshima brings the war to an end. My father resigns his position and accepts an offer to move to Venezuela to be an employee with the Mene Grande Oil Company.

1946: Mother continues: "In 1946 Dad went to Venezuela and you went to Hamilton Jr. High. You broke your arm, leg and back that year. You were a brave little fellow and so good to do the grocery buying and helping me. Before you and I went to join Dad you decided you wanted golf clubs so you caddied at a gold course with a steel brace on your back.." My mother and I fly from Houston to San Tomé, Venezuela. The trip takes three days via Mexico City, Guatemala City, Managua, Panama City, Baranquilla, Caracas, Barcelona, and finally San Tomé.

1947: Mother continues: "For two years, 8th and 9th grades, you were in San Tomé, Venezuela. Voted the best liked boy in the whole school. Do you remember your motor scooter? It was fun for me too as you would take me to the library at the club sitting behind you. Your English teacher (Miss Kennedy) raved about your anthology you wrote in the 9th grade. Smart, we thought you were. And still think so, even if our ideas are very different." Best friend is Carlos Garcia. He and I explore the surrounding towns and county side via my motor scooter. Learn to dance in the local bordellos with the young prostitutes and at the country club with my mother's friends. Drink a lot of rum and coke.

1948: My favorite teacher, Miss Kennedy, assigns the class to create an anthology of their favorite literature. I take this assignment seriously and devote a vast amount of time and energy to it. Type out the entire book. Read James Jones' *From Here to Eternity* and am greatly impressed by it. Later meet him and his wife, Shirley, in Paris and he gives me his old rain coat which I wear for years (until it falls apart).

1949: Graduate from Junior High School and win a watch as the "Outstanding Student". Elect to attend a boarding school, Georgia Military Academy in College Park, a suburb of Atlanta, because a friend from Venezuela, James Estrada, is a student there. (Later James is killed in a military jet accident.) Share a room with Louis Saladino, who is from New Orleans.

1950: Active in the literary activities of the school, but slip out and go over the wall at every opportunity. Often caught and forced to spend free time walking around "the bull ring". Spend all school holidays in Louisiana and Texas with aunts and uncles and cousins. Summer holidays in Venezuela with jobs with the oil company.

1951: Editor of the school yearbook and near the top of my class academically, but the lowest possible military rank.

1952: Almost am expelled from G.M.A. for breaking school rules (i.e. slipping out at night to meet local young women). But manage to graduate. Enroll in Louisiana State University in Baton Rouge in September. Become a member of Delta Kappa Epsilon social fraternity and live in the Deke House and also in the International Students House. Continue to travel to Venezuela every summer.

1953: My second year at L.S.U. – also known as the country club of the South. Attend classes, chase women, drink beer with friends. What a life! Pure joy! Go to Venezuela in the summer and have a job connected to the oil industry. Dance with the young prostitutes in the local bordellos. Deep sea fishing and swimming near Porto La Cruz.

1954: Live in a small apartment off-campus with Michael Meade Evans. Read Henry Miller's *Tropic of Cancer* and find Miller and his book a challenge and a major influence. (Read *Tropic of Cancer* again in Edinburgh in my 20s, again in London in my 30s and again in Paris in my 40s. Same book, different me. Each time greatly enjoy the experience.)

1955: Spend part of the summer as a chaufeur for my father's favorite cousin, Dayton Haynes, driving him around West Texas, Oklahoma, Colorado. (My "uncle" later sells his family home in Midland, Texas to the Bush family. Therefore it can be said that George W and I have slept in the same house. For whatever this is worth.) Enter L.S.U. that autumn with a sense of foreboding and a desire to drop out and explore options. After about a month in the university, leave with no clear plan. Uncle Sam sends me "a Greetings letter" requesting my services in the army. After taking the physical examination in New Orleans, am told to report in two weeks time to an army base in Arkansas for basic training. Walk down Canal Street, the main street in New Orleans, and see a poster declaring "Fly with the American Air Force". An hour later I have enlisted in the U.S. Air Force (for four years) and am told to report for basic training in Lackland Air Force Base in San Antonio in two weeks time. After thirteen weeks, sit in front of three men who decide one's fate. I express an interest in learning the Russian language and am assigned to Kelly Air Force Base just down the road. There I study Russian for six hours daily. And begin a friendship with Francis Randall, from Shreveport, and Morris Sheppard, from Cleveland. Many trips to Mexico. Via my "uncle" Dayton Haynes, I am introduced to Nancy Achning and her family. They are very warm and hospitable. No longer wishing to let *Kismet* decide my future, I track down the unknown corporal, Sonny from Mississippi, who will decide my future. He tells me he can send me anywhere in the world. I ask for Western Europe, in the smallest possible military base, near a major city and university. He suggests Edinburgh. Also in San Antonia listen to an Edith Piaf LP for the first time. Greatly impressed and become a fan..

1956: I arrive at Kirknewton in the autumn just after the Budapest Uprising and the Suez Canal catastrophe. Maybe World War III is at hand. Same night I arrive, I dress in civilian clothes that I had packed in my duffel bag and head for Edinburgh some fifteen to twenty minutes away. Immediately walk about the university area and fall in love with the city, a love affair that continues to today. Kirknewton is a small listening base where planes never land or take-off. Instead it attempts to learn all it can about the Soviet Union and its military plans and operations. Straight away request a meeting with the Base Commander, a Colonel Scott. Request permanent night duty

(5 to midnight), permission to attend the University of Edinburgh and permission to live in a small room in Edinburgh at my expense "in order to study". Bingo! Permission granted. My first room is in Great King Street. Later the landlady asks me to leave because I have had too many guests. An early encounter with Tamara Alferoff, a student from England, walking down Hanover Street that is to have future ramifications. Purchase a Volkswagen from savings from the summer jobs in the oil fields in Venezuela.

1957: Attend classes at the university and become involved with student life. Favorite professors: George Shepperson, who teaches American and Commonwealth History, and John Macintosh, Political Economics. Friends include Stash Pruszynski, from Warsaw, and Rod Macdonald, a Scottish-American. My first Edinburgh Festival. During a fringe production of Ugo Betti's *Corruption* in the House of Justice, spot a lively young man sitting in the same row. He is with two lovely companions. Afterwards see them again walking up the Royal Mile. Stop and offer them a lift. It is Ricky Demarco, his wife, Anne, and Anne's sister, Elisabeth. The beginning of a fifty year friendship.

1958: Meet Eva Clara Viveka Reüterskiold from Stockholm. She is in Edinburgh as an au-pair to improve her English. Live in the basement of 1, Doune Terrace and share the space with Ben Lassers and John Macnaughton – both medical students. Ben is from San Francisco and John is from Boston. Still travel to Kirknewton every afternoon, listen to the Russians and the Soviet states, drive into Edinburgh after midnight, sleep in Doune Terrace, attend classes the next morning. Party a lot with Ricky and Anne Demarco. Another Edinburgh Festival!

1959: Request permission from the Base Commander for a one-year early release from my contract with the U.S. Air Force and to my pleasant surprise, this is granted. Request permission to be de-mobbed in Scotland and permission from the British government to be allowed to stay in Edinburgh to continue my studies. Also granted. My family urges me to return to the USA and an American University. My father promises to support my studies in America, but will not help if I stay in Scotland. Drive to Spain in the Volkswagen and take the car to Majorca where I study at the University of Barcelona Summer School program. Meet Mother and Father in Barcelona and we drive to visit Jean Dacquin in Aix-les-Bains in the east of France. Then up to Edinburgh. Witness Father throw his KLM ticket from Barcelona to Edinburgh in the trash. Instinctively fish it out. Visit America in the summer and ship the Volkswagen there in order to sell it. I have decided to return to Edinburgh to continue my studies and to open a paperback bookshop to pay my cost of living. Total capital about 600 pounds. Before leaving New York, see *The Three Penny Opera* with Lotte Lenya. Return to Europe on the *Flandre* and experience the delights of France. Exit the ship in Southampton and go straight up to Edinburgh. Explore the university area and find a junk shop. Ask the proprietor if she would like to sell her shop and to our mutual surprise, she agrees to part with the shop and all the items in the shop for 300 pounds. Meet two people on a bus one morning and tell them my plans to open a bookshop. One is Jane Quigley (who is later to become a major actor in theatre, film and television using the stage name Jane Alexander) and the other is a fellow named Red Williams (who later tragically dies young). Red offers to help me. And soon after this meeting, The Paperback Bookshop is ready to open. Professor Alan Thompson cuts the ribbon. It is a perfect location and an immediate success with students, professors, and book lovers everywhere. The London publisher, John Calder, is one of the first to pay a visit. Our fifty year friendship and close association begins. The Paperback sells British and American paperbacks, literary magazines and the hip New York newspaper, *The Village Voice*. John Wilcock, an English journalist who was one of the founders with Dan Wolf, Ed Fancher, Norman Mailer, writes a weekly column entitled "The Village Square". I write a fan letter to John and tell him that I sell the newspaper in my bookshop. This begins a friendship which leads to a number of co-operative activities including The Traveler's Directory which later is re-named The Hospitality Exchange.

1960: The Paperback is a big success. Another trip to Spain with plans to continue to North Africa. Somehow get stuck in Seville and end up staying with the Sanchez Pizjuan family. English classes in exchange for a small room and meals. Somehow or other remember the KLM tickets I fished out of the trash in Edinburgh. Train to Barcelona. The ticket is still valid. My father and I have the same first name. Fly KLM back to Britain. The Paperback not only sells tickets for fringe productions, but I help create the first fringe catalogue. I am asked by the Edinburgh University Students Union to give the Address of Welcome to the new students arriving for the autumn academic year. Everyone seems to enjoy it and I am asked to do it every year for the next half dozen years. (Lynda Myles later tells me over dinner one night in Paris how inspiring she found my welcoming talk.) Create a theatre space in the bookshop and the First Dialogue by David Hume *Concerning Natural Religion* is organized by and performed by Dieter Peetz and becomes the hit of the 1960 Edinburgh Festival. Colin Hamilton and Peter Findlay also perform. ("The eighteenth century ambiance was created effectively in one corner of the bookshop, the rest of which was well filled with an audience who doubtless envied the performers their claret. But excellent coffee was provided to the entire audience afterwards. A discussion followed and when I left it was in full swing. This is probably the contribution of the Festival which owes more than any other to Edinburgh. It can be strongly recommended to anyone who enjoys a good Scottish argument." F.C. reviewing for *The Scotsman*) Jane Quigley is the star of the hit play in the fringe, Tennessee Williams' *Orpheus Descending*. I am an off-stage recorded voice shouting "Rope, get rope". Meet Scott Griffith in The Paperback. He is a young student from North Carolina studying at Edinburgh University summer school. Scott, Alan Daiches, Stash Pruszynski, Andrej Malczewski, and a fellow known as Highland Jim dig out the basement and it becomes a tapestry and pottery gallery. Breyten Breytenbach has his first exhibition of paintings in the gallery. Jane and a few friends depart for the International Youth Jamboree in Moscow. I want to join them, but cannot because of my military clearance. Decide to drive to the Book Fair in Frankfurt. This is the beginning of a long association with the city and the Book Messe.

1961: Learn in the summer that Viveka is pregnant and we get married in the Unitarian Church just before she returns to Stockholm to finish her university studies. The burning of *Lady Chatterley's Lover* outside The Paperback Bookshop by a former missionary in Africa is captured on film by Alan Daiches. John Calder organizes a tour of Britain for three French writers he publishes and John asks me to arrange a literary evening for Nathalie Sarraute and Marguerite Duras. The success of this tour leads John to suggest to Lord Harewood, the then Director of the Edinburgh International Festival, to add a literary element to the Festival. Harewood agrees with one stipulation: it must not lose money. John asks me to handle the Edinburgh end of the operation and he and Sonia Orwell, George's widow, start inviting novelists. I find local hosts to accommodate our guests to save spending money for hotels. Also make party arrangements and negotiate with the University of Edinburgh to use the McEwan Hall for the conference and the Men's Union for the daily lunches. The Paperback produces a review from Trinity College, Dublin for the Festival directed by Max Stafford-Clark. I publish Hugh MacDiarmid's essay on David Hume in an edition of 1000 copies.

1962: Viveka returns to Edinburgh and our son, James Jesper, is born the 20th of February in the Royal Infirmary. Our friend, David Baird delivers. We live at 63 Frederick Street and this becomes the office of the Writers' Conference. Organize a poetry reading for Yevgeny Yevtushenko that is a big success. Viveka cooks a dinner for Yevtushenko. Among the guests are Sean Hignett, a novelist from Liverpool but who lives in Edinburgh, Cesar Lopez, a young poet from Cuba, Alan Daiches, a photographer living in Edinburgh and Serge Lentz, a journalist from *Paris Match*. Serge writes a big article about the dinner party. And uses a wonderful photograph by Alan Daiches. Create *The Howff* at 369 High Street as a second theatre venue in Edinburgh with the folk-singer, Roy Guest. One is not supposed to speak ill of the dead. But the project ends after the festival when Roy leaves town with all the money. This leads to a talk with Tom Mitchell about a building he has acquired in the Lawnmarket and I suggest to him that we create a theatre club in his building and that we rent the space for one shilling a year. And he will serve as Honorary President. (Note: Tom, an English farmer, spends a great deal of time in Edinburgh as a direct result of meeting Tamara Alferoff, this same Tamara I met when I arrived in Edinburgh in the mid-50s.) Another production in the Paperback Bookshop, Fion McCulloch's *Trial of Heretics*. The first Writers' Conference at the Edinburgh Festival with 70 novelists in attendance (including Henry Miller, Lawrence Durrell, Norman Mailer, William Burroughs, Krushwant Singh, Angus Wilson, Mary McCarthy, Niccolo Tucci, Alex Trocchi, Hugh MacDiarmid, Alek Stefanovic) is a big success. Joan Hills asks if her husband, Mark Boyle, can have an exhibition in the Paperback Gallery. I suggest she wait and have it in the Traverse when it opens. Viveka, Jesper and I travel to the USA in order to introduce Jesper to my parents. We cross the Atlantic in a Norwegian tanker. Rough seas in the winter.

1963: The Traverse Theatre Club opens its doors in January and I miss the opening production. Visit with Jane Quigley in New York. She is now acting under the name of Jane Alexander. See her in *Man is Man*, an off-Broadway Bertolt Brecht production. Beg her to pack her bags and come back to Edinburgh to join us at the Traverse. But she has been offered a major role at the Charles Playhouse in Boston. (And besides British Equity would never have allowed her to perform at the Traverse.) The Traverse rapidly goes from strength to strength. John Calder, Kenneth Tynan and I co-organize the Drama Conference at the Festival with 120 people connected with the theatre in attendance. On the last day, the theme is "The future of the theatre" and a happening is organized by Charles Marowitz, Allan Kaprow, Ken Dewey, Carroll Baker and others in which a nude model, Anna Kesselaar, is quickly wheeled across the organ gallery. Outrage and scandal. The Lord Mayor of Edinburgh refuses to allow us to organize a Poetry Conference for 1964. Somehow manage to purchase a large apartment at No. 4 Great King Street and it becomes the office for The Drama Conference.

1964: For a brief period, I am both the Artistic Director and Chairman of the Board of Directors of the Traverse. Manage to establish the policy that the Traverse will be the home of new writing, that we will create a school of Scottish playwrights. The Arts Council insists if they are ever to give us any funding, I must resign one position. I give up the Chairmanship and urge the members to elect Nicholas Fairbairn, a local flamboyant lawyer, to serve as Chairman. He is duly elected. And I see my position weaken immediately as a result. Create Traverse Festival Productions to produce the English-language premiere of the Bertolt Brecht/Kurt Weill musical, *Happy End*, in the Pollock Hall during the Festival. It is the hit of the Festival and later transfers to the Royal Court Theatre in London. Jack Henry Moore, a young American from Oklahoma who is working as a Private Detective in Dublin, knocks on my door. He is a theatre director and has read about me and The Traverse in *The Observer*. He travels to Edinburgh to see *Happy End* and to ask me for a position at the Traverse. I cannot hire him because of British labour laws, but an almost 40 year friendship begins. Travel to Dublin to spent a week at the Dublin Theatre Festival and to share the city and festival with Polly Grannis and Jack Moore. Meet Lindsay Kemp who is penniless and we raise money to cover his expenses for him and his small dance company to return to England. Later he comes to Edinburgh and Jack and I produce his next half dozen productions in the Traverse (and later in the Arts Lab in London). Viveka returns to Stockholm to live and takes Jesper with her.

1965: A banner year at the Traverse and at the Paperback Bookshop. The success of *Happy End* produces an invitation from the official festival to produce one of the principal dramatic pieces for this year's Festival. Make a list of twelve possible plays we could produce and all are refused. Finally ask the Festival which Shakespeare play they would like to see us do. They suggest *Macbeth* and we agree to produce it. We need the money. Michael Geliot directs and it features three young, attractive and nude witches. More scandal! In the Traverse itself, we launch C.P. Taylor with the World Premiere of his *Happy Days Are Here Again* (directed by Charles Marowitz). Also produce the first production of *Oh, Gloria* by Robert Shure. I am asked by Penguin Books to edit a book for them of Traverse Plays. I am also awarded the Whitbread Prize "for outstanding contributions to theatre in Britain". Bernard Cassen, a professor in Paris, writes an article for *Le Monde* about the Traverse. Am invited to present a Season of Traverse productions in the Arts Theatre in London. A critical success. But not a financial one.

1966: The year begins with a brilliant production of the musical, *The Fantastiks*, directed by Jack Henry Moore. Even his detractors are impressed. This is followed soon after by another World Premiere of C.P Taylor's *Allergy*. Next the World Premiere of Heathcote Williams' *The Local Stigmatic* (suggested to me by Harold Pinter). And a friendship begins with Heathcote Williams. But my situation in Edinburgh is in difficulty largely due to a growing dislike of Jack Henry Moore and his open homosexuality. (If one were a homosexual in those days, it was required to stay in the closet. One certainly didn't flout it.) The fact that I wish to open a sister theatre in London, so that productions can go back and forth between the two cities, is another reason the Committee is upset. In the end I painfully resign from the Traverse and move to London. The London Traverse Theatre Company (with support from Jennie Lee, the Minister of Culture, and Arnold Goodman, an important lawyer and later the Chairman of the Arts Council) is created. The other three directors are Charles Marowitz, Michael Geliot and Ralph Koltai. Manage to "rent" Sonia Orwell's basement flat for the princely sum of serving drinks at her many cocktail parties. Sonia introduces me to Frances Bacon, Cyril Connolly, Stephen Spender and most of the social and political power of London. The London Traverse has a brilliant season with highly critical reviews for all our productions. Two productions, *The Bellow Plays* and Joe Orton's *Loot*, transfer to West End theatres. Both plays are directed by Charles Marowitz. *Loot* wins the *Evening Standard's* Best Play of the Year Award. Thanks to Michael White, Yoko Ono produces her first happening in our theatre. With a borrowed five hundred pounds from Victor Herbert, a friend in Paris, we (Jack Moore, Barry Miles, John Hopkins, Michael Henshaw) launch a newspaper called *International Times*, later shortened to *I.T.* I borrow the Round House in Chalk Farm from Arnold Wesker to have our *I.T.* launch party. Hoppy arranges for the Pink Floyd and the Soft Machine to play. This party also launches the Round House as a space for creative endeavors. Give theatre tickets to Norma Moriceau, a waitress from Sydney, and we become (and still are) dear friends. Norma becomes Fashion Editor of *19* and then returns to Australia to become a film set and costume designer. Other Australians in London include Richard Neville, who starts the hip magazine, *OZ*, at about the same time we launch *I.T.* Martin Sharp, a painter, also from Sydney who greatly contributes to *OZ*'s success. And of course Germaine Greer, who is outrageous and wonderful and one of the most articulate human beings I have ever encountered. Felix Dennis, who is not Australian, joins *OZ* and helps with the distribution. He later creates a global publishing empire and becomes amazingly rich. He uses a large percentage of his wealth in his attempt to re-forest Great Britain.

1967: Move to Long Acre in Covent Garden. Share the flat with Jack Moore and thousands of others. We have a pay phone installed and everyone comes for tea and/or to use the telephone. More and more disappointed in the Jeannetta Cochrane Theatre and the restrictions and pressures of running a theatre company in a large conventional space. I resign in order to devote myself to *I.T.* and to finding a warehouse in which to create an experimental space. Soon manage to acquire the perfect space – two warehouses connected to each other at 182 Drury Lane. This is the birth of the Arts Laboratory. The Lab contains a cinema in the basement designed by Jack Moore and run by David Curtis. The entrance contains a large gallery space and Biddy Peppin (David's girlfriend) and Pamela Zoline direct the gallery activities. The theatre is in a separate (but connected) warehouse and it is designed by Jack Moore. He and I co-direct the activities there. The upstairs space in the front contains the restaurant that is run by Susan Miles. I live in the back above the storage and dressing rooms. A number of other people live in various corners of the building. We are everything we claim to be and the space is an instant success. All London comes at all hours to experience The Lab. My policy is to try to never say the word "no" and in three years of running the Lab I almost never do so. We have a number of successes including Steven Berkoff's first production, a Kafka's adaptation, Graziella Martinez and Toni-Lee Marshall's late night dance production, Jack Moore/Jack Bond's direction of the Jane Arden musical, *Vagina Rex* and the *Gas Oven* (with music by Shawn Phillips), John Lennon/Yoko Ono's sculpture exhibition, Jack Moore's direction of Tutte Lemkov in Kafka's *Lecture to an Academy* and Moma Dimic's *The Very Long Life of Tola Manolovic.*. David Bowie uses the Lab to rehearse his music. Lindsay Kemp stages many productions. So, too, The People Show. Meet Ernie Eban when he walks into the Lab and our friendship begins. Also friends with the Topolski clan. Meet Hercules Bellville. Meet Dick Gregory and a long and warm friendship begins. Later I am his European Campaign Manager when he stands for President of the United States. Meet James Baldwin. Meet the American Ambassador to Great Britain, David Bruce, and his wife, Evangeline. Meet the Cuban Ambassador, Madame Alba Griñán.

1968: Our newspaper, *I. T.*, creates UFO where the Pink Floyd and The Soft Machine are the house bands. Jack creates The Human Family and begins to spend more and more time touring Europe with his bus, geodesic dome and his actors. More and more of the staff and personnel in the Lab resent scarce funds being spent on him and his activities on the continent and not on the Lab itself. Ultimately and painfully I side with Jack. This causes a major eruption and some of the staff break away to create another Arts Lab. Am invited to participate in a conference in Florence entitled, "The Problems of the Small Theatre". Invited by Frank Burckner to bring a production to his Forum Theatre in Berlin for a festival of international theatre. Elect to produce *The Party* and I call a bunch of actors and musicians and tell them we are going to Berlin to have a party. It is a big success. In April, the London production of *Hair* uses the Arts Lab to audition actors. Drive to Paris in May with the writer, Philip Oxman. Find myself caught up in the "revolution". Standing outside the Odeon Theatre when it is seized, I am among the first dozen inside. We drive to Geneva and continue to the South of France and discover the Cannes Film Festival has been cancelled. Meet Austryn Weinhouse, the translator of de Sade into English. On my way back to London, stop in Heidelberg and end up staying the night in the house that Albert Speer built. And he is somewhere in the house. But we do not meet. The May 13th issue of *Life* has an article about the Arts Lab by Horace Judson entitled Arts Laboratory: Swinging Smosgasbord. At some point, I meet Lynne Tillman at Shakespeare & Co in Paris and invite her to come to London and to assist me in the running of the Arts lab. She accepts and soon is contributing her positive energies to the Arts Lab. In December, we hire the Albert Hall to organize a fund-raiser, *The Alchemical Wedding*. John Lennon and Yoko Ono participate with their bag happening. An evening to remember but the management of the Albert Hall is not amused. I had promised Leonard Cohen. He didn't come. The event is taped with one of the first Sony video cameras. Inspire and help Tony Elliot to launch *Time Out* in London. Party with Jay and Fran Landesman, Ronnie Laing, Christine Keeler, Mama Cass. Am invited to dine with Brian Epstein and The Beatles. Also invited to dine with Indira Gandhi. Meet Leonard Cohen earlier via Michael X. Leonard and I discuss

114

starting an egg-head paperback publishing company together. Viveka and I divorce. She wants to marry someone in Sweden.

1969: Squat the empty Bell Hotel next to the Arts Lab after all attempts to rent it from the Greater London Council fail. Shortly afterwards we are expelled by the police. Some say this is the start of the squatting movement. Last year of the Arts Lab in London. The writing is on the wall. But one of the interesting things about the Arts Lab is the number of other Lab-like places that explode all over Britain and the Continent as a result of the example the Lab's success provided. Places like the expanded I.C.A. in London (under the direction of Michael Kustow), the Milky Way in Amsterdam (where Jack Moore is one of the founders), the Entrepôt in Paris (where Frederic Mitterand shows me around when it is an empty shell), plus hundreds of Arts Lab in Britain itself. At a Sunday afternoon tea with Bill Levy, we decide to create a sexual freedom newspaper to be called *SUCK* and to be based in Amsterdam. A quick telephone call to Willem de Ridder in Amsterdam and he agrees to be the paper's graphic designer and to host the operations in his own newspaper office. Make a few more telephone calls and Germaine Greer and Heathcote Williams join the team. Accept an invitation from Professors Pierre Dommergues and Bernard Cassen to become a Visiting Professor at the newly created University of Paris 8 in the Bois de Vincennes. Teach summer school in Granna in the South of Sweden. Move to Paris and stay the first three months in Victor Herbert's large apartment at 6 rue du Val de Grâce in the 5th arrondissement. With luck manage to move to rue Mathurin-Régnier in the 15eme. Begin teaching in the autumn in Paris. Extremely large classes. Pierre Dommergues suggests I might need an assistant. Mollie Lehberger is assigned the position and a friendship with her and her husband, Martin, begins. Thanks to a letter from Peregrine Eliot (containing a check), we are able to "roll the presses" for the first issue of *SUCK*. Take copies of *SUCK* to the Frankfurt Book Fair and sell it in the aisles. This is my second Book Messe and I am to attend every year thereafter. The *Suck* editorial board decides to create The Wet Dream Film Festival to open after next year's Frankfurt Book Fair. I am to be the Director. Bill Levy meets Susan Janssen when preparing the first issue of *SUCK*. (They still live together some 35 years later. They also co-produce Swaantje, a wonderful daughter.) Susan and Lynne Tillman actively contribute to the success of SUCK Begin to write newsletters that I send out to friends all over the world. (In 2005, the number of newsletters has exceeded 630.) Viveka marries Gosta Wallmark, an architect.

1970: Cover the Cannes Film Festival for the *L.A. Free Press*. Make publicity for The Wet Dream Film Festival and solicit films. Am invited to continue teaching at the University of Paris and discover I enjoy teaching. (In the end I stay on the staff at the University of Paris 8 for the next 29 years until I am forced to retire at the age of 65, mainly teaching "Media Studies" and "Sexual Politics".) Another Edinburgh Festival. Another Frankfurt Book Fair. The first Wet Dream Film Festival in Amsterdam is a big success. We don't lose money and everyone enjoys the event. The beautiful model, Jean Shrimpton, adds beauty and glamour by attending. She and Heathcote are close friends. Develop a close relationship with my neighbor in Paris, Elahé Arouzi Ebtehaj. She is from Iran and lives across the street from me with Sitare Agaoglu, a student from Istanbul. Also becomes friends with Susi Wyss, one of the great beauties and free spirits of the time. Susi later becomes a neighbor. I have the pleasure to dine often in her apartment.

1971: More teaching, more SUCKs, another Cannes, another Edinburgh, another Book Fair, another Wet Dream, and an invitation to participate in a conference, The Doom of the Book?, in Zurich. A trip to the USA where I meet Robert Crumb in San Francisco and Henry Miller in L.A. Henry Miller asks me to contact Jens Jorgen Thorsen when I am back in Paris and to tell Jens that Henry greatly enjoyed his film, *Quiet Days in Clichy*. I do and Jens and I become friends. Also meet Betty Dodson in Manhattan in Fred

Jordan's Grove Press office and ask her to be a Jury Member for the 2nd Wet Dream Film Festival. She accepts and a wonderful friendship with her begins. Viveka and Gosta have a daughter, Lisa, in March. Jack Moore and the Videoheads crew move from Amsterdam to my atelier and a long relationship with UNESCO and Sony (Mr. Baba and Mr. Shoda) begins. Meet Suzanne Brogger at Cannes and talk her into writing an autobiographical story for *SUCK*. With Garry Davis, we produce a World Passport. I use it to travel from Switzerland to Italy and on to France. Spend some time with Germaine Greer in Italy and with The Rolling Stones in the South of France. Wet Dream Film Festival is a big success once again. Sign a contract with Grove Press for my book, *Hello, I Love You!*

1972: More of all of the above. Disastrous film project (Wet Dreams) with Max Fischer that has some positive aspects. One is a short film made by Jens Jorgen Thorsen. Travel to New York City to meet with Grove Press for my book, *Hello, I Love You!* Meet Jeanne Pasle-Green at a Manhattan party and invite her to co-edit *Hello* with me. *SUCK* commits hara-kiri. Many reasons. But the film project with Max certainly a factor. Cannes again where I see the first screening of W.R. – *Mysteries of the Organism* with Dusan Makavejev and four friends. Dusan moves from Belgrade to Paris and lives one street away from me. He and his wife, Bojana, become good friends. Another Edinburgh Festival, another Book Fair. Will Reed uses our World Passport to get out of prison in Bangkok and to travel over land to Paris. I put him up in Paris, feed him, introduce him to many people, help him financially. This later leads to a disaster. My home is a World Government Embassy that never closes as more and more people knock on my door at all hours to be issued World Passports. I am asked to produce a theatre production for the Olympics in München and pass the job to Jack Moore. But I do travel to München just before the Games begin to visit with Jack and the company. When I leave to fly to Paris, I am stopped at the air port with fifty blank World Passports in my carry-on bag and spend the next two hours lecturing to the police about World

Government. In the end, issue a passport to one of the custom police and am allowed to continue on my way.

1973: Thanks to Mike and Martine Zwerin, I move to 83 rue de la Tombe Issoire. They move to the South of France and I manage to take over their rental contract from the American poet, Lloyd Frankenberg, and his wife, the painter, Lorin McIver. Henry Miller lived just up the street in Villa Seurat when he published *Tropic of Cancer*. Attempt to launch an audio magazine, *The Cassette Gazette*. John Lennon and Yoko One express a great interest in the project. Mick Jagger makes a financial contribution and contributes a Revox tape recorder. The first issue contains Lawrence Ferlinghetti reading one of his poems and Charles Bukowski reading one of his stories. The Bukowski contribution is a gift from his friends, Bob Head and Darlene Fife, who edit *NOLA Express* in New Orleans. Ferlinghetti later tells me that he started publishing Bukowski in City Lights because of *The Cassette Gazette*. Attend a UNESCO Conference on experimental education in Hamburg (thanks to Judith Bizot) and give a paper suggesting the creation of a Ship University. Afterwards everyone is excited about the project. Attend another UNESCO Conference on "drugs" in Paris. Become involved with a crazy airline project, "Freelandia" that ends in a mess. Not mine fortunately. Another Cannes Film Festival, Edinburgh Festival, Frankfurt Book Fair.

1974: Grove Press backs out of the *Hello* contract and Praeger agrees to publish. Then Praeger decides the book is too hot to handle when the Berger Supreme Court changes the censorship laws in the U.S. The French government charges the World Service Authority (and Garry Davis and yours truly) with three counts of criminal activity. The trial takes place in Mulhouse and two charges (counterfeiting and fraud) are dropped. Only charged with "confusing the public" (which is what advertising agencies do every day). We are found guilty and my relationship with the World Government movement semi-ends. Garry elects to continue and moves to Vermont. Publish one thousand copies of *Hello, I love you!* on a duplicating machine and everyone who visits is encouraged to collate a book..

1975: Almonde Editions is founded and 600 copies of *Hello* is printed. Travel to the USA with my wonderful son, Jesper. Attend a strange luncheon in Neuilly and meet Gunnel Bloomberg. This develops into a very close friendship. More university classes, Cannes, UNESCO, Sony, Edinburgh, Frankfurt. A note from Samuel Beckett to thank me for sending him a copy of *Hello, I Love You!* I dine from time to time with Beckett when his London publisher, John Calder, visits Paris.

1976: All of the above continues. Lenny Jensen lives in atelier and launches the A2 Cable television station for our neighbors. He also co-produces a beautiful daughter, Jessica, with Marie-Paule Etienne. *Hello* is translated and published in Italy by Angelo Quattrocchi. Sitting one night late in *La Coupole* develop an idea with Humbert Camerlo to send several Beaux-Arts marching bands around the USA to celebrate the 200th anniversary of the founding of the United States. Humbert and I organize the tour and he goes on it. I don't. He reports it is a wonderful experience..

1977: Attempt to write a book about *La Coupole* to celebrate its 50th birthday. But fail to get permission from Pierre Laffon's brother. Introduce Jack Moore to neighbor, Quentin Rouillier, and this leads to a dance production in the Paris Opera House entitled *Wind, Water and Sand* with Caroline Carlson and Quentin as the principal dancers. Dandelion Editions is created and it prints and publishes my little manifesto, *Workers of the World, Unite and Stop Working!* With luck and with a lot of help from friends (Bo Linden, Annie Gruska and Gilles Bouchez), manage to purchase my atelier. Videoheads and Jack Moore move their base of operations from my atelier to a converted bank in Amsterdam. Videoheads is invited to assist the Cannes Film Festival by videotaping the press conferences. Norma Moriceau and Lisa Brody are our camera team.

Travel to the Edinburgh Festival with Lisa Brody and Baya Müller. Jill Fenner and Benny Young read excerpts from *Hello, I Love You!* in the Traverse bar. Maurice Hatton cajoles me into participating in his film, *The Long Shot*, in which I play the role of Jim Haynes. After the festival, attend a Conference on Love and Attraction in Swansea with Lisa and Baya. Stay with Sally Belfrage in London after Swansea. Two delightful weeks in Manhattan the end of September. Another Frankfurt Book Fair. In December, thanks to Yvonne Rockman, make a trip around the world. (First stop Bombay to see Pearl Padamsee and am guest of honor for a party of New Delhi theatre school graduates at Neelam and Pushpinder Chowdhry's home, then Sydney to stay with Norma Moriceau, Melbourne next to stay with Yvonne and Irvin Rockman. Irvin is the Mayor of Melbourne.)

1978: End 1977 with a fantastic party at the Rockman's and begin the New Year in Melbourne by making love with a beautiful Melbourne woman. Continue to Hong Kong, Seoul, Tokyo, L.A. (where I stay with Bernie Cornfeld), Houston (where I stay with my mother and father), New York City, London and home to Paris and university classes. *Workers* re-published. Another Cannes. Another Edinburgh Festival and the World Premiere of Long Shot. Another Frankfurt Book Fair, Then a trip to Bavaria to be a witness for the defense in Raymond Martin's obscenity trial over his distribution of *SUCK* in Germany. We win. (Raymond publishes three of my books in German-language translations.) Cathy Sroufe arrives in Paris and thanks to Colette Négrier, she stays in Atelier A2 and we begin the dinners that are to become a fixture for the next three decades Cathy also stays in Paris, marries Yves Monnet and they co-produce *Charles and Arthur...*

1979: Ulli Lindenmann lives in Atelier A2 and knits me a wonderful blue sweater. Meet Barbara Crighton, from Toronto, in Shakespeare and Company and she moves into Atelier A2. Cathy Sroufe and I seriously develop the Sunday Salon project and every week more and more people call to invite themselves to dine. Most of the profits are later used to send food, clothes and medicine to friends in Poland and other places in Eastern Europe. The Bank, a video access center, opens in Amsterdam under the direction of Jack Henry Moore and Videoheads. Cannes again. Edinburgh Festival again. The entire November issue of the German-language magazine, *Pardon*, is devoted to fullering. I begin to correspond with Jill Diamond in the Women's Prison in Rennes. Martin Lehberger moves into atelier A2. Challenge a *Time Out* in London critic to a debate in the I.C.A. when he gives *Workers* a bad review. He accepts. Go to London and win the debate and he acknowledges/apologizes.

1980: Handshake Editions founded the 29th of February in response to Ted Joans being invited to read at UNESCO and his needing a book of poetry to sell after the reading. His book, *Duck-butter Poems*, is the first of many titles published over the next twenty-five years. (Others include books by Michael Zwerin, Judith Malina, Lynne Tillman, Sarah Bean, Tom Dunker, Yianna Katsoulos, David Day, John Calder, Pablo Armando Fernandez, yours truly.) Dick Gregory flies to Paris and then to Teheran in an attempt to free the hostages held when the Embassy is seized. Dick asks me to serve as his contact in the West when he calls me every day and I call on another telephone to his wife, Lilian, in Chicago. This means that I miss my annual trip to Cannes and postpone a trip to the USA in order to assist Dick. Meet Ali Alizadehfard and Flanagan MacKenzie. Later manage to come to their assistance in Marbella when I arrange for them to meet Benny Puigrefagut. Go to the Edinburgh Festival and help Cathy Sroufe Monnet with her dance presentation in Herzmark's Dance Centre. Henry Miller dies and I get a note from Phillippe Coupey asking what we will do about Henry. Decide to publish a Homage to Henry and Philippe's letter is the first contribution. Organize a big press conference for Dick Gregory at Charles de Gaulle airport when he returns from Teheran. Rush back to Paris from the Edinburgh Festival to arrange this. Visit Jill Diamond in the Women's Prison in Rennes on her birthday the 2nd of December and we meet for the first time. Vangelis asks me to sing and to organize a chorus to sing the title song for his next LP, *See You Later*. Arrange for a tall blonde Californian, Pauline Kouweonhoven, to teach him English.

1981: My mother has a "routine operation" and dies in the hospital. Rush to Houston to be with my father. He wants to sell his home and move to Louisiana. Rent a small truck to help him move his things to Shreveport. Am hit by a car on an overpass while still in Houston and almost lose control of the truck. It would have meant a sure death. The car that hits me does not stop. I continue the drive, but am extremely shaky. Arrange for Jack Moore to marry Yoko Toda in New York City. Handshake Editions publishes *Everything Is!* and it also comes out in the German-language. Paula Klein, from Stuttgart, knocks on my door. She ends up living in A2. Attend another Edinburgh Festival. Meet Jane Dalrymple in Edinburgh and she briefly visits afterwards. (Much later am responsible for her meeting Anselm Hollo. They marry and are still together.) Also another Frankfurt Book Fair. Rent a car and travel from Frankfurt to Berlin with Catherine Hilliard and Daniel Topolski (and stay with Inge Krahn). Continue to Poznan and Warsaw. Re-new friendship with Barbara Hoff who I first met in London in Indica Bookshop in 1967. Attend The Jazz Jamboree in Warsaw. Meet Pawel Brodowski, the Editor of *Jazz Forum* and a long friendship ensues. Drive to Prague with a letter to be delivered from Andrzej Blikle and Solidarnosc to Vaclav Havel. Meet Ivan Havel and am told his brother is in prison.

1982: Use the small profits from the Sunday dinners to send packages of food, clothes and medicine to friends in Poland. Handshake Editions publishes Judith Malina's book of poetry, *Poems of a Wandering Jewess*. A quick trip to Louisiana to spend some time with my father. Travel to Manhattan to see Jesper, Lynne Tillman, John Flattau and Betty Dodson. Betty challenges me to a wager as to whom will publish their autobiography first. The loser has to fulfill the winner's sexual fantasy. Drive to Cannes with Dan Topolski and Catherine Hilliard for another Film Festival. Stay once again in the Regence Hotel. Odile Hellier opens her wonderful English-language bookshop, *The Village Voice*, on the 14th of July. (Some 25 years later, it is still a great bookshop.) Dorota Janiszewska, from Warsaw, but studying at the University of Paris 8 moves into Atelier A2 thanks to Jessica Ben John. Gordana Malesevic moves into A2 for a year. She is from Stockholm. Another Edinburgh Festival. Stay with Barbara and Scott Griffith in their wonderful William Street Lane Mews home (and continue to stay there until they sell this house and move to the South of France in the Spring of 1992). Prepare 25 copies in two volumes of a "participatory autobiography" and take ten copies to the Frankfurt Book Fair. Thanks to Fanny Dubes, Robert McCrum, Elisabeth and Jaco Groot, Faber & Faber elect to publish it. But when I travel to London to sign the contract, Robert and Matthew Evans demand more words from me. Fanny helps make it happen. Travel to Warsaw for another Jazz Jamboree.

1983: Spend a lot of time at the Cannes Film Festival with Shuji Terayama. He and I first met in London in the Arts Lab and a close friendship evolves. Good friends in Paris, Hamida and Colin Gravois, co-produce another daughter, Kenza. Hana was born in 1981. Another Edinburgh Festival, Frankfurt Book Fair, Warsaw Jazz Jamboree. And Sunday dinners. More and more people want to attend.

1984: Faber & Faber publish my autobiography, *Thanks for Coming!*, in London on the 13th of February. And later they publish it in the USA as well. Faber throws a big party in London for about 300 to 400 friends. Peter Hillmore writes something in *The Observer* about the party and I am pictured with Pete Townshend. Generally the book receives good reviews. Attend the Cannes Film Festival in May once again for the *L.A. Free Press*. Debate in the Oxford Union the motion "that this house regrets the passing of the 60s" and my team wins. Ernie Eban coaches me and he and Ulla Larsen come up to Oxford to cheer me on. Handshake Editions publishes *Powered Punch* by Yianna Katsoulos. Another Edinburgh Festival! Another Frankfurt Book Fair and another Warsaw Jazz Jamboree. Kyle Roderick writes an article about me entitled "20/20 Haynes-Sight".

1985: One of the first articles about the Sunday dinners is written by Margaret Austin for London's *Cosmo*. The article produces nice visitors from Britain. It's May, so Cannes again. Then in June am invited to the Lahti Writers' Reunion in Finland by Juhani Seppanen. (This literary meeting becomes a fixture and I attend another seven times. Meet and become friends with Liisa & Tim Steffa, Matti Rinne & Tuula Isoniemi, Karolina Blåberg, Pentti Holappa, Esa Sariola, and so many others.) Bo Akermark writes an article about the Sunday dinners for Stockholm's *Dagens Nyheter*. Make my first trip to Russia in October thanks to Carol Pratl. Fly from Paris to Leningrad with a group of friends (Ulla Larsen, Lisa Nesselson, Layne Jackson, Jean-Pierre Remonde, Lydia Caldas and my wonderful dentist, Sylvie Daniel). Meet Anna Luna in the street. Train to Moscow and Ulla insists we smuggle Anna in our compartment. Stay with Julia Watson and Martin Walker. Bribe a train conductor to take Anna back to Leningrad. Yevgeny Yevtushenko cooks dinner for Martin Walker and me in his dacha in Peredelkino.

1986: My father dies the 21st of January in a hospital in Haynesville, Louisiana and is buried next to my mother in a local cemetery. The end is very sad and disturbing. But once my mother is no longer alive, my father seems to lose his desire to carry on. I understand this is common. Another very busy year. James Atlas writes an article about literary Paris for *Vanity Fair* and mentions Handshake Editions. Barry Gifford writes about Odile Hellier and *the Village Voice* Bookshop and my small role there. Make a trip to Eastern Europe and also go to Cannes again. Plan an unusual literary happening with Carsten Hansen for the Arhus Festival in September involving calling a dozen writers and having our conversations listened to by an audience. Dahn Ben-Amotz writes a profile of me for a paper in Israel. Another Edinburgh Festival. Favorite production is the Mario Vargas Llosa's *Kathy and the Hippopotamus*, directed by Stephen Unwin at the Traverse. I meet Vargas Llosa and find him to be warm and open. My ex-atelier mate, Anna Kohler, perfoms with the Wooster Group. The *Financial Times* Drama Critic, Michael Coveney, suggests I see *5 Screams* by the Tmu-Na dance theatre company from Israel. I do, greatly enjoy their performance and then help arrange for them to tour America. A strange aspect of this visit to Edinburgh is my ability to pay taxi fares with copies of my autobiography, *Thanks for Coming!* Ricky Demarco opens his new gallery in Blackfriars Street. Travel next to Arhus for our happening. The co-host, Lally Hoffmann, and I talk with Arnold Wesker, Mario Varas Llosa, Manuel Puig, Wolf Bierman and others…Cathy Sroufe Monnet has a son, Charles, with Yves Monnet the 24th of September. There is a big article in the *L.A. Times* (The Third Wave) about Americans in Paris. Good friend, Bernard (Willem) Holtrop, has a drawing in *Liberation* dealing with the *L.A. Times* article. Another Frankfurt Book Fair and another Warsaw Jazz Jamboree. Participate in a Conference on Alternative Lifestyles in Manhattan organized by Russ Weis.

1987: Peta Zabiego opens her restaurant, Rose Blue, and my small investment helps make it happen. Another Cannes Film Festival. The second Lahti Writers' Reunion. John Fowler writes about Lahti in the Glasgow Herald. Fly to Warsaw from Helsinki. Another trip to Poznan and to Warsaw. Michael Gross writes about Paris fashion for the *New York Times* and mentions me. An article by Heike-Melba Fendel and a provocative photograph of me sitting on a large motorcycle with Heike's beautiful legs resting on my shoulders in *Playboy Deutschland*. Another wonderful Edinburgh Festival. See Damian Cruden superb production of *Marlene: Falling in Love Again* and decide to take it to Paris. Anne Marie Timoney transforms herself into Dietrich. Talk with Marlene herself on the telephone and invite her to the Premiere. She declines but asks for two tickets for friends. Also remind her that we met when she sang at an Edinburgh Festival (in 1961 I think) and I went up to her dressing room and knocked on her door and the two of us talked for about thirty minutes.) Christopher Hudson writes a piece about me for the *London Standard*. Go to Frankfurt Book Fair. Then to another Warsaw Jazz Jamboree. Continue to Belgrade for the October Meeting and on to Budapest.

1988: Invited by Lou Casimir to lecture at Bucknell University. Another Cannes Film Festival. Corine Berrevoets moves into A2 and paints the guest room. Sharon Shuteran & Peter Muckerman have a son, Eliot Paul, the 8th of June. Joyce McMillan writes a history of the Traverse Theatre that is delightful. I write an "Open Letter" to her to correct a few mistakes. Another Edinburgh Festival. Stephanie Wolfe Murray picks me up outside Filmhouse in her car, suggests we go for a drink. The results is my *People to People* travel series of books for Canongate. Another Frankfurt Book Fair. Another Warsaw Jazz Jamboree. Talk Jim Campbell into attending. He and I also attend the October Meeting in Belgrade. Moma Dimic invites me. His play, *The Very Long Life of Tola Manolovic*, was a hit in the London Arts Lab, directed by Jack Moore and performed by Tutte Lemkov. Train to Ljubljana to be with Nevenka Koprivsek. Then fly to Warsaw from Budapest and sit across the aisle from Gabor Betegh and Agnes Sandor – two students I met on the same flight one year earlier. Travel to London to attend and to help publicize Jan Kaczmarek's *Orchestra of the 8th Day* concert at Queen Elizabeth Hall. (In 2005 Jan wins an Oscar for his original music for the film, *Finding Neverland*.) On Sunday morning, the 17th of November, decide to bike to Alesia for the London newspapers. A shopping bag gets caught in the front wheel and I end of breaking both arms. Very silly. Very stupid.

1989: Trips to London, Los Angeles and Berlin. Cannes once again. My third Lahti Writers' Reunion. Edinburgh Festival. Frankfurt Book Fair. Warsaw Jazz Jamboree and stay with Barbara Hoff.

Take Corine Berrevoets to Warsaw. Serve on the Jury of the Charles Chaplin New Directors Award (with Percy Adlon, Forsyth Hardy, Janos Rosza, Susannah York and Krzysztof Zanussi) and we give the prize to an Indian, Shaji, for his film, Piravi (The Birth). The 2nd Prize goes to Ildiko Enyedi for her film, *My Twentieth Century*. She is from Budapest and I later meet her there via Janos Xantus. Belgrade October Meeting. Begin to develop the *People to People* travel series. Poland is first and the easiest to produce.

1990: February trip to Berlin for the Film Festival, continue to Budapest for another film festival where I meet András Barabas and András Török. Prague next. Mike Zwerin writes an article for the *International Herald Tribune* about my *People to People* project. Eric Bergkraut writes an article about the Sunday dinners for a Swiss newspaper. John Flattau has an exhibition of his photographs in the Galerie Agathe Gaillard in Paris. There is an article in the London Times about Jane Alexander and yours truly. Once more manage to attend Cannes, Edinburgh, Frankfurt and Warsaw festivals. One of the great publishers of the 20th century and a dear friend, Maurice Girodias, dies while being interviewed for an Israeli radio station. David Applefield publishes the guide book, Paris Inside Out, and writes kind words about me. Jack Moore develops a film about Marlene Dietrich. I manage to get a VHS videocassette copy to Gilles Jacob thanks to Pascale Dauman. He loves the film and wants the film to open and/or to close the Cannes Film Festival. But we need to clear a lot of rights before the film can be screened.

1991: Another year of travel. Cannes in May. Fourth Lahti Writers' Reunion in June. August in Edinburgh. A September trip to Arhus. Another visit to Warsaw and the Jazz Jamboree, up to Gdynia for a Polish Film Festival. Also go to Berlin and Madrid. In between all this manage to continue teaching at the University of Paris and to host Sunday dinners. Also go to Bucuresti and meet Roxana & Dima Bicleanu, Leo Serban and many others. Read friend Alan Furst's novel, *Dark Star*, and am knocked out by it. A reception for

Lynne Tillman and Susan Mancur is held in A2 to celebrate the publication by Serpent's Tail of their two books. The Warsaw Voice reviews my *People to People: Poland* book. Dora Puszta and Monika Vig, from Budapest, visit me in Paris and interview me for the newspaper, *Hungarian Orange*. Monika is the Editor. Later Monika is tragically killed in an automobile accident. Born 2 Nov 1966 – died 5th Sept 1992. Dora and I become good friends. She is extremely helpful with the *People to People: Hungary* book. We visit each other often. Jesper visits Rio and stays with Katherine Hilliard. Joe Francis lives in the upstairs guest room. Ghazi Imraish also stays in the atelier. And Jack Moore is in the basement. Roxana and Dima Bicleanu, who were my hosts last July in Bucuresti, come and visit and help with the *People to People: Romania* book. I recommend Linda de Nazelle for a role in a French film entitled *Border Line* and she gets the part.

1992: The magazine for the *Independent on Sunday* publishes a three page rave review of the *People to People: Poland* book. The Montreal Gazette writes warmly of the *People to People: Poland* book. The *Sydney Morning Herald* has an article about the Sunday dinners. My legal problems with Emile Gouiran get more complicated and I curse the day I ever walked into his office. Travel to Budapest, Bratislava and Prague in April. Learn while staying with Eva Kacerova in Prague that Marlene Dietrich has died. Rush to Paris and down to Cannes and call Gilles Jacob, the Director of the Festival. Tell him I am in Cannes with a videocassette of Jack Moore's tribute to Dietrich. He says he will call me back within 24 hours. He does and says that it is too late to arrange a screening. I rent a videocassette machine and a monitor and arrange with the Majestic Café to screen the film at midnight, using their space and electricity. About 200 people stand outside in the softly falling rain to watch and to cheer the film. Bill Russell writes in *The Herald* that he saw the best film of the Festival standing in the rain at midnight outside the Majestic Café. Introduce Bill Bryden when he gives a talk in *the Village Voice*. Travel to the Baltic Republics. Am awarded a prize in

London by Nicholas Albery and the Institute for Social Inventions for the *People to People* guides. (Nicholas is later killed in a stupid car accident.) Edinburgh Festival in August. Another Frankfurt Book Messe. October trip to Prague with John Flattau and Arne Lewis. Zephyr Press in Boston announces the first four *People to People* titles. .

1993: In February, travel to the Baltic Republics and on to Russia. Am profiled in *The Moscow Times*. The Managing Editor is a friend, Meg Bortin. The Polish Institute in London organizes an event for the *People to People: Poland* book. Stephanie Wolfe Murray and her Publicity Director, Jamie Byng, attend. In April 1993 travel to Russia again. My little manifesto, *Workers of the World, Unite and Stop Working!*, is translated into Russian by Yuri Golitsinski and published in Saint Petersburg thanks to the New York poet and friend, Marco Polo. Meet Alex Kan in St. Petersburg and he interviews me for a Russian magazine about the *People to People* series. Attend the Congress, Erotica 93, in Bologna, Italy. Travel to Amsterdam to see Bill and Susan Levy and to visit The Bank. Cannes again in May. My essay. "On Being Lazy" is translated and published by Leo Serban in Bucuresti. Fifth Lahti Writers' Reunion and travel to St. Petersburg. Attend a poetry reading to celebrate Yevgeny Yevtushenko's 60th birthday. He reads before 5,000 fans. Afterwards we dine in a private room in the Astoria Hotel with the Mayor (Sobcheck) and his Assistant. I talk briefly with the Assistant and little do I realize that I am talking with a future Czar of Russia, Putin himself. He is laconic, asks if I speak German and apologizes for his "bad English". Moscow afterwards. Edinburgh Festival in August. A September trip to Vilinus, Moscow, St. Petersburg, and back to Vilinus. Organize a photographic exhibition in St. Petersburg for John Flattau. October another Frankfurt Book Fair and organize a party in the Künstlerkeller. Travel to London in October. Publish a Mary Guggenheim novel, *Love in the Minimalist Mode*, in Handshake Editions. Print it in Vilnius thanks to help from Almantas Samalavicius.

1994: A February trip to Berlin, Prague and Budapest. Help publicize Bob Kingdom's one-man performance, *The Truman Capote Talk Show*. John Flattau finds and faxes me an article in the *New York Post* about the New York District Attorney looking for Emile Gouiran. Lyle Stuart writes in his Hot News about my introducing him to Samuel Beckett in the Boulevard Raspail. I am asked by the London production of *Hair* to write a programme note. My dear friend in London, Sally Belfrage, tragically dies far too young. April trip to Berlin, Warsaw, and Vilnius. April trip to London. Write a letter of support to Professor Ma in Seoul. Create a Handshake Editions catalogue. Apply for a Guggenheim grant. It is refused. Edinburgh Festival in August. Stay with Stephanie Wolfe Murray. Twelve city tour in the USA to promote the *People to People* series. Stay in Chicago with Samantha Stenzel and she and Frank Sherman arrange for me to meet Studs Turkel and to be interviewed by him. It is a second time. The first time was in London in 1968. My hostess in San Francisco is the beautiful Swede, Lotte Jonsson. Stay with Kyle Roderick and Brett Goldstone in L.A. Another Frankfurt Book Fair and host another Kunstlerkeller party. Trip to Athens to organize a photographic exhibition for John Flattau. Travel to Spain to spend New Year's Eve with Victoria and Benny Puigrefagut.

1995: Travel to Morocco to surprise Laura Corsiglia and Ted Joans. Stay with them another week in Rabat and other cities. February trip to Warsaw and stay with Barbara Hoff. A trip to the south of France to visit Barbara and Scott Griffith in their new home. Guggenheim Foundation letter again says "no". Am interviewed by Ruth Bonapace and it's published in the United Airlines in-flight magazine. Organize an exhibition for John Flattau in Budapest and we travel there. Sixth Lahti Writers' Reunion. Continue to St. Petersburg. Anne Hoenig visits and she and I travel to London. Catherine O'Sullivan gives me an affidavit about Emile Gouiran that she later retracts. Edinburgh Festival in August. Stay for the first time in Martin Burke's superb apartment at 84 Great King Street. (And Martin lets me stay every year afterwards.) Stephanie Wolfe

Murray and I host a superb party. Frankfurt Book Fair and another Kunstlerkeller party. A December trip East to Warsaw.

1996: Travel with Kyle Roderick Goldstone to Milano (and stay with Sasha Stefanovic & Claudio Innocenti) and on to Athens. Kyle is researching a biography of Gregory Corso. I warn her about Gregory and tell her that it could end badly. And it does. Gregory withdraws his support. John Calder publishes a sweet article about me in the *Magazine Litteraire* in Paris. There is an article about the *People to People* series in a Zagreb literary magazine. Someone takes a wonderful photograph of Laura Corsiglia, Ted Joans, Kyle Roderick and yours truly in the *Café La Roquette* in Paris. Trip to Warsaw for an exhibition of John Flattau's photographs at old friend, Stash Pruszyski's restaurant. I am asked by Galya Ackerman to find a first class accommodation for the President of Lithuania, Vytantas Landsbergis, for his visit to Paris and to organize a cocktail party for him. Stanley Cohen agrees to host the cocktail party. Invite Galya Uchayk and her friend, Leni Miasnikova, to Paris. And they have a great time! The jazz singer, Katia Lubinsky, is a house guest and we become close friends. Another Edinburgh Festival and another festival party co-hosted by Stephanie Wolfe Murray and yours truly. Frankfurt Book Fair and Kunstlerkeller party. Ennio Marchetto performs in Paris and I assist with the PR and attend almost every night and push hundreds of friends to attend. Amanda Hootan writes a profile of me for *The Scotsman* magazine that cuts me up in little pieces and spits me out. Not nice. I travel to Havana with John Flattau. And attend the Havana Film Festival.

1997: Marion Winik writes a wonderful article that is published in the American Air Lines in-flight magazine about the Sunday dinners. Katia sings at *Blue Note* in Paris. Emile Gouiran writes me one of his awful letters. Decide to write a one-sentence book entitled *Women's Liberation: A Definition* and it will contain this one sentence on every page in a different language. Plus a footnote of a few sentences dealing with the verb, "to assert". (The sentence: Women's

Liberation is the recognition by both women and men of the need and the right of each and every woman to assert herself.). Book never finished. Trip to Athens for John Flattau's exhibition. Wonderful time with Alexandros Lykourezos, Alicia Coriolano, Renos Mandis and John Zervos. Travel to Luxor in March with Linder Allen, Jack Moore, Meg Bortin to explore the possibilities of creating a production company that would develop a theatre. Handshake Editions publishes David Day's collection of poetry entitled *Just Say "No" to Family Values*. Seventh Lahti Writers' Reunion and afterwards continue to St. Petersburg and Moscow. Travel to Madrid in July and stay with Menchu Gutierrez. Another Edinburgh Festival and festival party. Another Frankfurt Book Fair and Kunstlerkeller party. Write an article for Howard Aster on John Calder that is published in a Festschrift honoring John. Lisa Nesselson writes a poem, Emile the Rat, for my birthday. Yun Wu visits from China (and St. Petersburg) and I take her to Hamida & Colin Gravois' Xmas party.

1998: Trip to Istanbul with John Flattau. I stay in Muge and Semih Sokmen's publishing house (Metis Publications) in Beyoglu, in the center of Istanbul. Sean Hignett visits Atelier A2 and writes an article for *The Telegraph*. Travel to London to participate in The Free Speech Wars Conference. Assist Howard Aster in the preparation of a Festschrift for John Calder. Linder Allen organizes a benefit auction to help raise money for my legal fees in my fight with Emile-the-Rat. Bob Gross is the auctioneer. Learn that ESSEC has Emile-the-Rat teaching Business Ethics in their Law School. He is soon fired when the school realizes his past. Harry Robinson takes some wonderful photographs of the Sunday dinners. Another Edinburgh Festival and another festival party co-hosted by Stephanie Wolfe Murray and me. Trip to New York City and meet with the District Attorney and we discuss Emile Gouiran. They say they still want him for his past activities in America. Another Frankfurt Book Fair and Kunstlerkeller party. Take Katia Lubinsky to Amsterdam and stay with Xaviera Hollander. Paula Klein, Dorota Chrisp and John

Flattau send an open letter to many of my friends seeking financial support to help me pay my legal bills and the letter raises over $30,000. The French Bar Association disbarment of Emile Gouiran happens!

1999: John Lloyd writes an article for the *Financial Times* about me and my problems with Emile Gouiran. Get a threat fax signed "a friend" that comes from Emile-the Rat's fax machine. Attend the London Book Fair with Howard Aster. An April trip to Athens. Eighth Lahti Writers' Reunion. Plan to create a Paris Arts Club like the original Traverse Theatre Club. Frankfurt Book Fair and Kunstlerkelle party. Article in the Dublin Irish Independent by Jonathan Bowman about the Sunday dinners. (He later falls down stairs in his home and is tragically killed.) The American Center in Paris and its sale is a scandal that is waiting to explode. I ask the American Center Foundation for help in creating a Paris Arts Club in the rue Nevers, but am refused all assistance. Write a Letter to the Editor to the *International Herald Tribune* in November attacking the concept of "art", but letter is not published.

2000: Begin to find members and funds to purchase the rue de Nevers space. It is an almost perfect location and space. Get a letter and affidavit from Donna Gouiran about her ex-husband, Emile-the-Rat, and Catherine O'Sullivan. Try to make a deal with the Michelin Corporation to use/acquire a small museum they own near UNESCO. No success. An article in the Italian magazine, Panorama, about the Sunday dinners. Write an article for Caledonia Magazine entitled Three Days in My Life. Continue to raise money to purchase the rue de Nevers space. Sabine & Rainer Kölmel call from München to say they will help. And they do! Make another trip to Havana in April for John Flattau's photographic exhibition that I co-organize with Pablo Armando Fernandez, a poet and dear friend since our first meeting in 1961. I fly from Paris and John flies from New York. Joan Bakewell makes a television documentary about the people who changed Britain in the 60s and comes to Paris to interview me. Later Terry O'Neill photographs Tariq Ali, Neal Ascherson, Margaret Drabble, Ned Sherrin, Jonathan Miller, Ruth & Richard Rogers, Alan Sillitoe, Joan Bakewell, Beryl Bainbridge and yours truly for The Sunday Times magazine colour supplement. Attend the last night's performance of Gay Marshall's musical, *If I Were Me*, in a small theatre in Paris and offer to help her get it produced in the Edinburgh Festival. It becomes one of the hits of the Festival in the Assembly Rooms. Edinburgh Festival is once again sensational and Martin Burke is not only my host again, but he co-hosts a party with Stephanie Wolfe Murray and me. Another Frankfurt Book Fair and another Künstlerkeller party. Malcolm Brown writes a superb article about the Sunday dinner parties for the KLM in-flight magazine, but the editor cannot use the piece because of some sexual references. The film-maker, Jens Jorgen Thorsen, dies and I write an obituary about him for the *London Independent*. Organize a big New Year's Eve party in the rue de Nevers space. There is a large colour photograph of David Turner and yours truly in a magazine called *Living in France*. We look like Robert Redford (David) and Clark Gable (me). Judith Wardle writes an excellent article that goes with the photo. (Maybe she took the photo as well.)   .

2001: Travel to Glasgow in February to produce my happening in the Tramway. Brief visit with Ruth Holloway and Martin Burke in Edinburgh on my way home to Paris. Write an essay about the beginnings of the Traverse for their web site. David Langford writes an article about his friendship with Martin Lehberger and the Sunday dinners. Go to Scotland again in August for another Edinburgh Festival. A heart attack while watching the press screening of *Le Fabuleux Destin d' Amélie Poulaine*. End up in the Western General Hospital. One telephone call to Sheila Colvin and the word immediately spreads all over Edinburgh, to Paris, to London, to New York City, to L.A. and elsewhere. Telephone calls, visitors and flowers begin to arrive. Beautiful flowers from Mary Shields, Bill Burdet-Coutts and all at the Assembly Rooms. Also flowers from

Larkin McLean and her mum and dad. What a time, place and way to end one's life. But with excellent treatment I recover. Thank you, Dr. Denvir. Am allowed (reluctantly) to check myself out just in time to attend a lecture by Gore Vidal at the Book Festival. Simon Pia writes a gossip item about this for *the Scotsman*. Keith Bruce and *The Herald* honor me with a Little Devil. Martin Burke is a perfect host once again. Return to Paris via London and a few days with Ernie Eban. The World Trade Center disaster unfolds. Another disaster follows when my almost 40-year friendship with Jack Henry Moore begins to come unstuck. (Not the time and place to analyze here.) Acquire a doctor in Paris. Meg Bortin's suggestion. Frank Slattery is from Dublin, did his internship in Paris, fell in love with the city and is still here twenty something years later. He prescribes 6 pills daily. I am allowed to travel to Frankfurt in October for another Book Fair and another Kunstlerkeller party.

2002: Attend the Prague Writers' Conference in April with John Calder. Thank you, Vlasta Brtnikova and Michael March. Meet the wonderful Ivana Bozdechova., who teaches at Charles University. Also meet Elmore Leonard and his wife, Christine. This leads to a meeting with Gregg Sutter and Amy Alkon. Mischa Richter borrows my atelier for a fashion shoot for the magazine, I-D, in London. Four extremely beautiful blonde models interrupt my life for two days. They are wonderful! Alex Ninian writes an article about the Sunday dinners for the *Chicago Tribune*. Another Edinburgh Festival in August. In September, the atelier becomes a gallery and the first exhibition features the paintings of James Mitchell. James King has the next exhibition, followed by Audren Thorez's "Chubby Ladies". The Frankfurt Book Fair in October and host another party in the Kunstlerkeller. Thanks to Natasha Perova, three of my books are back in print again: *Everything Is!*, *Workers of the World Unite, and Stop Working!* and *Round the World in 33 Days*. Trip to Manhattan in November to stay with my son and with John Flattau. John and I fly to Guadalajara to attend the Book Fair with Howard Aster. Cuba is the Guest of Honor. Howard and I have co-published, *Parables, a*

Spanish/English bi-lingual edition of Pablo Armando Fernandez's poetry. Pablo also attends the Book Fair and we manage to spend a lot of time together. Back in Paris, fly to Edinburgh in December for the 40th Anniversary birthday party of the Traverse Theatre.

2003: In the A2 gallery, host an exhibition of paintings by a neighbor, Trish Nickell. Next Harold Chapman's "The Beat Hotel" photographs, followed by Ewa Rudling's photographic portraits. Then paintings by Antonio. In April travel to Timosoara and Cluj to attend a Goran Bregovic concert, thanks to Maria Rankov, and it is one of the best concerts I have ever attended. The death of old friend Ted Joans in Vancouver. John Calder writes a moving obituary for *The Guardian* that I frame and keep in the atelier. Sylvie Beach Whitman organizes a week long Writers' Conference to celebrate Shakespeare & Co and she invites James Emanuel, Jake Lamar and yours truly to celebrate Ted Joans' life and poetry. We do and it is a very moving tribute. Go to the Edinburgh Festival and manage to talk Varda and Ami Ducovny into coming as well. They have a great time. Sad to report but Ami dies when they are back in Paris. Another Frankfurt Messe and another Künstlerkeller party. Ride there with Howard Aster and he begins to discuss the possibility of editing and publishing a Festschrift honoring yours truly. John Flattau and I fulfill our promise to Susi Wyss when we take her to Prague in November.

2004: The twins, Slobodan and Vladimir Peskirevic, have their paintings in the A2 gallery, followed by Jesper's photographs of attractive young women in urban situations in Tokyo, Bangkok, Stockholm, etc. Next exhibitions : Robbie Conal's political caricatures followed by Antonia Hoogewerf's Indian photographs. Am invited to be photographed by William Klein and it is published in Max in France. Travel to Milano to stay with Alek Stefanovic and to be with John Flattau, Joanna Przybyla and Sasa and Claudio Innocenti, An article in the *Financial Times* about my reading tastes. Edinburgh Festival again. Spend a lot of time with Joan Bakewell.

Julia Watson writes an article about yours truly. Adrian Leeds writes a piece about the Sunday dinners. Spend some time with Cara Black in Paris and tell her I love her murder mysteries all set in Paris. John Morrison interviews me about the Edinburgh Festival. Frankfurt Book Fair and Kunstlerkeller party in October. Mary Bartlett, Cathy Monnet, Antonia Hoogewerf and I decide to co-edit a cook book with the possible title, *Cooking for 100 – Dinner in Paris with Jim*. Take a leaflet to Frankfurt and distribute to many publishers. Howard Aster makes a leaflet about the Jim Haynes Festschrift which he displays at the Book Fair. Organize 65 friends to see the Cole Porter film, *De-Lovely*, in a small Paris cinema. Carol and Lyle Stewart tell me not to miss the film. Also Lisa Nesselson. Everyone loves the film! Viveka and Gosta visit me in Paris. She is as beautiful and wonderful as ever.

2005: Sabine Kölmel's paintings cover the walls of the A2 gallery at the start of the year. David Turner's photographs of the many people he encountered on his trips to Japan, Istanbul, Egypt, etc is next. Travel to India in February with Antonia Hoogewerf. Dolly Thakore hosts a party in Mumbai for Antonia and yours truly. We travel next to Calcutta and are joined by Karolina Blåberg and Martin Lehberger. Stay in the Fairlawn Hotel and meet old friend, Sanjeev Prakash. Next travel by train to New Delhi. Dine with Neelima and Pramod Mathur. Neelima introduces me to Gandhi's grandson, Ramchandra, and to her own son, Varun, and daughter, Reeti. Alladine Lacroix flies in from Paris. Then in March I go to Barcelona with John Flattau. Back in Paris, am sent two copies of the school text book where my essay, "We are not on earth to suffer" is published by Belin. Kids in France who study English might learn other things as well. Raise some money for Lucy Allwood's film, *My Sister Vazimba*. (Harry Robinson, Colin Gravois and I each invest 500 euros.) Dine with John Calder (on the 30th of April) and with Antonia Hoogewerf and Karolina Blåberg. John suggests at that dinner I might write a year by year synopsis of my life for the Festschrift. Then on the 2nd of May, Howard Aster calls from Toronto to say that he plans to send the Festschrift to the printers the end of May in order to have it ready in August for the Edinburgh Festival. I mention John Calder's suggestion. Howard thinks it is a great idea and a great addition to the book. Now some weeks later, I hope everyone thinks it's a great idea.

Like Piaf, no regrets. OK, maybe one or two. Why did I loan Will Reed 500,000 francs (which he never repaid, not even one penny). This same Will Reed I saved (with Garry Davis) from a prison in Bangkok. And why did I accept Will Reed's recommendation to use Emile Gouiran as my lawyer? Using Emile is like accepting a dinner invitation from a cannibal and agreeing to be the meal itself. Was my heart attack a result of all the angst and pressure of this crazy and stupid action on my part? Why did I purchase atelier C5 and put it 50-50 in Corine Berrevoets and my name? And then later agree to sign over my 50% to her in order to hide the property from Emile? When she moves to the suburbs with the father of her children and I suggest we sell the atelier, she claims I gave it to her. A total loss.

I regret the loss of my friendship with Jack Henry Moore. I keep thinking it could have been avoided, that there is no reason why we should not still be friends and supportive of one another.

But on the positive side of the ledger, I have so much to be thankful for. A great son! Good friends, of course! Pretty good health all these years. Reasonable intelligence. Passion. The love of and for women. My love of people. My optimism and enthusiasms. It's a great life so far. Long may it continue.